CW0054891B

CONTENT

1945–1975

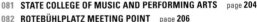

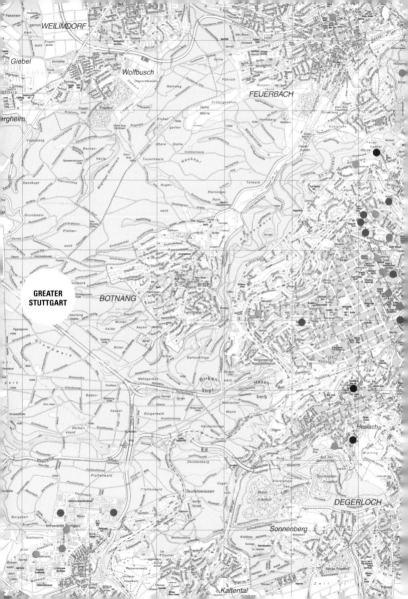

FOREWORD

The built environment can only be perceived by walking through a city with eyes wide open and an open mind. Buildings tell stories of their development, their inhabitants or their historical connections. The Stuttgart Architecture Guide was conceived for all those who are approaching Stuttgart for various reasons—whether as a resident, tourist or on business—and who want to learn more about the city's formative modern buildings, from 1900 to the present day. Reading this guide, the traveller will not only find out more about the outstanding achievements of building culture in Stuttgart, but also comprehend the threats, loss and decay to which they have so often been exposed over the past century.

There are many architectural highlights whose exemplary reputation extends far beyond Germany's borders, achievements that have had a lasting impact on international architectural culture. Stuttgart's modern architecture was most significantly affected by the 1950s and 1960s in post-war Germany. The Wüstenrot Foundation is grateful and proud to have been given the opportunity to support the production of this guide. One of the Foundation's primary concerns is to conserve and maintain the cultural heritage of our society, and to safeguard and embed cultural and artistic accomplishments in society's collective memory.

Particular attention is paid to emergent cultural values from the period after 1945, as they are often not considered worth preserving, thus putting them particularly at risk. By incorporating these buildings in this guide, we would like to contribute to their protection. Also, we would like to draw attention to the admirable Stuttgart architecture and encourage all readers to explore the streets of Stuttgart and engage in the stories that each and every building has to tell, for there is a Stuttgart of widespread constructed quality that makes the city an outstanding testimony to Germany's rich architectural heritage.

Philip Kurz, Wüstenrot Foundation

INTRODUCTION

   The Dukes of Württemberg chose a picturesque spot for their courtly 'stud garden' at the end of 10th century and for their residence in 1495. Enclosed by ridges on three sides, the cauldron-like restricting location did not prevent the dukes, and later kings, from erecting edifices that satisfied their urge for representation and public affairs for centuries with designs that followed contemporary architectural styles and incorporated state-of-the-art technology. From the 20th century onwards, Stuttgart's architectural avant-garde from time to time produced pioneering work that gave new impetus for national and international constructions. Some of these were acknowledged for their theoretical background and search for the right form, others received critical acclaim for their innovative technical or functional solutions. Just as the internationality of its planners is appropriate for the city's industry, commerce and visitors, the plurality of education and research at the University of Stuttgart has also increased. It is therefore all the more astonishing that there is no guide in English to Stuttgart's architecture in this modern period. Written to remedy this gap, this architecture guide is to be understood as a contribution towards an international dialogue about building culture. By no means all the buildings that would have deserved a mention made it into the guide.

The selection was guided by criteria like being accessible by public transport, at least visibility from the street and their proximity to other highlights. That is why only the primary authors' offices have been mentioned and not those of other contributors or sources of inspiration.

The guide is divided into six periods which follow the most important political turning points of the twentieth century: the period prior to the First World War, the inter-war period, and National Socialism. The period after 1945 is divided into post-1945 reconstruction, postmodernism and deconstructivism after 1975, as well as the reflexive modernism after 1990. Within the periods, the projects are in chronological order of their time of completion, not taking in account any preliminary competitions. The designers of the projects are named; unfortunately, space constraints meant that it has not been possible to mention other planners and engineers involved in the projects. The category 'nearby' refers to other interesting buildings in the vicinity of the respective objects and expands the spectrum of this guide.

Christiane Fülscher, Klaus Jan Philipp

Around the year 1900 Stuttgart, 'the city in the basin', was so built up that a further expansion could only be achieved by building extensively on the ridges. Fortunately for the city, in 1906, it was decided to not have any densely covered areas halfway up the hills but dispersed developments in the form of detached houses on large estates. The city owes its green character to this decision. Panorama roads offer magnificent views into the 'cauldron'. In 1908 a building exhibition on the site of today's castle gardens presented concepts for the further development of the hillside slopes.

A less forward-looking decision in an urban planning sense was to transfer the old railway station next to the Schlossplatz (built in 1844, façade of Georg Morlok from 1867 in Bolzstrasse 10) just 500 m down towards the Neckar. Though the main station was at the edge of the inner city at that time, it was already clear that the city would continue to grow along the roads leading to the Neckar and Heilbronn and that the mighty complex of the railway station would impede the extension of the city along the valley. Suburbanising Bad Cannstatt and villages like Feuerbach, Gaisburg, Heslach, Botnang and others, the city soon grew into a veritable metropolis.

The expansion of the inner city with buildings of cultural and administrative infrastructure reflected this new role: the opera and the theatre (Max Littmann, 1912) impressively span the upper castle garden. Their backs faced the boulevard-like Neckarstrasse (today Konrad-Adenauer-Strasse) lined with bourgouis city villas, the State Library, the State Archives and the (old) State Gallery (Georg Gottlob Barth, 1843). The column colonnade of the Königsbau (Christian Friedrich von Leins, 1859) at the head of the Schlossplatz befits the image and self-esteem of a major city. This building was flanked by the Kronprinzenbau (Friedrich von Gaab, 1842) with its neo-Renaissance façades, and the neo-Baroque Marquardt Building (Eisenlohr & Weigle, 1896).

In contrast to this, the neo-Gothic town hall (Jassoy and Vollmer, 1905) overlooking the market place was mainly surrounded by medieval buildings. The Haus der Wirtschaft (Skjold Neckelmann, 1896), the Alte Schauspielhaus (Albert Eitel, 1909) and many civil buildings in the west and south of the city centre are still testimony to the splendor of the Wilhelminian era. A first urban reconstruction (1909) around the Hans-im-Glück fountain went some way to restoring the medieval street situation.

001

BISMARCK TOWER
Bismarckturm

REALISED 1904
PLANNER Wilhelm Kreis
ADDRESS Am Bismarckturm 36
ACCESS Restricted

The Bismarck Tower is a memorial building erected on behalf of the students of the Technical College in honour of Otto von Bismarck, who dominated European affairs from 1862 to 1890. In line with his massive and rough presence as politician and his monolithic character, the building sits on the highest peak of the city and has a rather solid, plain design realised in coarse 'Stubensandstein'. The Bismarck Tower—one of 50 realised by Wilhelm Kreis Germany-wide—was reduced to a clean and technical construction based on a few geometric shapes. In line with the motto of Kreis' final design of 1899, 'Götterdämmerung' (twilight of gods), the Stuttgart memorial was used as a pillar of fire. A flame bowl superimposed on the top of the tower was lit for the opening ceremony and afterwards for commemorative events, such as Bismarck's birthday, his date of death and the anniversary of the 'Deutsches Reich'. In comparison to other contemporary memorial buildings, Kreis' Bismarck Towers advance more to a lithic architectural symbol than a memorial site for the statesman himself. In 1928 the tower was converted into a water tower.

NEARBY Roser Country House (1921, Bonatz & Scholer, Am Bismarckturm 58), Bonatz House (1922, Paul Bonatz, Am Bismarckturm 45)

CREMATORIUM OF PRAGUE CEMETERY
Krematorium Pragfriedhof

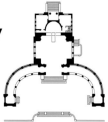

REALISED 1904–1907
PLANNER Wilhelm Scholter
ADDRESS Pragfriedhof
ACCESS Restricted

Entering the Prague Cemetery (edified in 1872) from the main entrance, the visitor passes the neo-Gothic administration building and chapel (1876) designed by August Beyer that constitute the prelude of the main axis leading to the great volume of the elevated crematorium. The unique building was based on Wilhelm Scholter's design from 1902. The architect proposed a symmetrical ensemble of a solid, soaring main volume containing the crematorium flanked by two arched colonnades closing to the rear with columbaries. Two pointed pavilions conclude the complex and house the wide-ranged stairs leading to the forecourt in front of the crematorium's entrance. The complex illustrates the contemporary monumental architecture by using decorative elements of neo-Renaissance, neo-Baroque and Art Nouveau as well as citations of old Egypt's architecture like the pyramidal roof and sarcophagus emblems that hide technical aspects like chimneys. Inside is a central quadrangular assembly hall with two adjoining side aisles and an apsis. A tambour with copular extend the centralised volume upwards providing additional light sources.

NEARBY Memorial 'Zeichen der Erinnerung' Nordbahnhof (Otto-Umfrid-Strasse)

003

HEUSTEIG SCHOOL
Heusteigschule

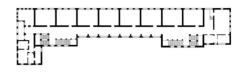

REALISED 1905–1906
PLANNER Theodor Fischer
ADDRESS Heusteigstrasse 97
ACCESS None

The school building in the south of Stuttgart is based on the design of the architect and urban planner Theodor Fischer, famous for his ambitions to re-form architecture and urban structures in a modern way and therefore a role model to his students and colleagues. Erected in 1905/06, the huge volume of the school structured its urban surroundings. The symmetrical building is divided into a main volume with four floors of classrooms in rows of eight and two side pavilions with five floors for staircases, staff rooms and offices. On the ground floor of the main building an arcade links the exterior and the interior. Lattice windows with and without arches and turret-like extensions on the hip-roof are the highlights of the otherwise simple building. Inside red clay tiles on the floors, blue tiles on the walls and wooden wardrobes painted violet make the visitor feel welcome. The school was to be a comfortable and useful one, which still can be seen and felt after its faithful restoration (1989–1991). This building served as a model for many subsequent institutions like the Leibniz Grammar School and the Lerchenrain school.

NEARBY Marienplatz (2003, Freie Planungsgruppe 7)

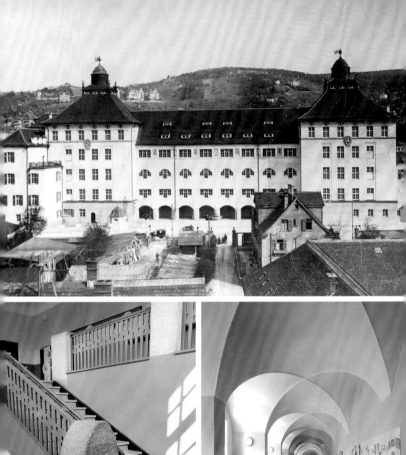

ST MARK'S CHURCH
Markuskirche

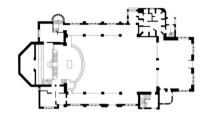

REALISED 1906–1908
PLANNER Heinrich Dolmetsch
ADDRESS Filderstrasse 2
ACCESS Open to the public

The protestant St Mark's Church was built between 1906 and 1908 by the architect Heinrich Dolmetsch, who was known as an expert for churches in the south of Germany. Positioned at the intersection at the side of the Fangelsbach cemetery, its main entrance marks the beginning of the Römerstrasse. Inside a barrel vault the nave spans almost 20 m, its arches merging with the wall pillars and visualising the support structure. Two lower and narrow aisles flanking the nave permit light to flood through huge, oval clerestory openings. The octagonal choir closes with the extended organ covering an assembly room underneath. Next to the main entrance is the square bell tower with its octagonal tambour and then round spire; cross and lion top the nave's red mansard roof. The façade is rendered, while the portal, the door and the window soffits as well as the pilasters displaying the bearing structure are of sandstone. Although St Mark's Church was one of the earliest church buildings—along with the Garrison Church in Ulm by Theodor Fischer (1910)—made of concrete, its formal language is rather traditional.

NEARBY Marienplatz (2003, Freie Planungsgruppe 7)

005

GRAF-EBERHARD BUILDING
Graf-Eberhard-Bau

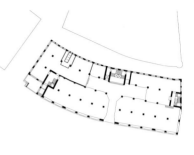

REALISED 1907–1908/1980–1982
PLANNER Karl Hengerer, Heinz Mehlin,
Karl Reissig/Walter Sorg
ADDRESS Eberhardstrasse 10–16
ACCESS Restricted

A slender tower with a pyramidal roof can be seen from many points of the city. This stair tower (with paternoster) and the Graf-Eberhard Building, for which it was designed, was the largest commercial building project of the city at the beginning of the 20th century. Two pediments left and right top the five-storey curved façade along the Eberhardstrasse, while the middle part of the building has dormers. Shops and a café with two-storey high windows open to the roadside. The windows of the upper floors are connected in groups of three, giving the façade its own rhythm. Though the façade is clad with natural stone the construction is of reinforced concrete and allows wide spanning distances. With its sparse ornamentation the building contrasts with the mock-medieval Geißstrasse-Quartier (Hans-im-Glück fountain) surrounding it. It clearly marks the beginning of modern architecture in the early 20th century. Together with Theodor Fischer (Art Building) and Paul Bonatz (Main Station), Martin Elsaesser (Market Hall), Karl Hengerer belongs to those architects who gave Stuttgart a metropolitan appearance in the years before WW I.

NEARBY Department store Galeria Kaufhof (1960–1961, Egon Eiermann, Eberhardstrasse 28), Gustav Siegle House (1912, Theodor Fischer, Leonhardsplatz 28).

LERCHENRAIN SCHOOL
Lerchenrainschule

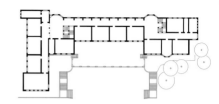

REALISED 1909

PLANNER Paul Bonatz

ADDRESS Kelterstrasse 52

ACCESS None

Located at the top of a steep slope in the south of Heslach, Paul Bonatz's first school building has a representative character. The architect used large terraces and staircases to manage the difficult terrain. The gym is partly built into in the slope and functions as a basement for the classrooms on its top. As it protrudes from the main wing into the main schoolyard, it forms a roof terrace—another schoolyard. On top of the gym sits the main volume of the building—three storeys high, used for classrooms and flanked by two head-end buildings. The layout facilitates best conditions for lighting and ventilation. The light-flooded corridors run parallel to the rows of classrooms. The setup is similar to the Heusteig school of Theodor Fischer and was used as a template for later school buildings in Stuttgart. Made of rough plaster, a decorative and abstract frieze and symmetric windows order the façade. The protruding sections at the corner of the head-end buildings are derived from the floor plan and house two staircases. The strong symmetry of the whole site is interrupted by a lower wing connected to the left head-end building.

NEARBY St Joseph (1975, Rainer Zinsmeister und Giselher Scheffle, Böhmis-reuteweg 19)

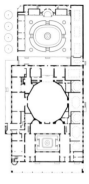

ART BUILDING OF WÜRTTEMBERG ART ASSOCIATION

Kunstgebäude des Württembergischen Kunstvereins

REALISED 1909–1913/1956–1961
PLANNER Theodor Fischer/Paul Bonatz, Günter Wilhelm
ADDRESS Schlossplatz 2
ACCESS Restricted

When the Lusthaus by architect Georg Beer (1584) burned down in 1902, Theodor Fischer was commissioned to replace it. He wanted to create a cultural building that opened a dialogue between the vertical structure of the Olga Building and the horizontal structure of the New Castle. Hence, he used thin columns for its vertical structure and an epistyle as well as a triangular pediment as horizontal elements. The front hall protrudes 2 m over the edge of the square and is lower than the New Castle to maintain the eye's focus. The dome with the golden deer on top denotes the old axis of the place, linking it to the Old Castle opposite. Inside, the art building is multifunctional, containing conference rooms, studios, a restaurant and space for exhibitions. The building's history is a turbulent one: built by Theodor Fischer, it was destroyed in WW II, reconstructed in a simpler way by Bonatz (he changed the thin columns of the front hall to thicker pillars with heavy capitals) and then extended by Günter Wilhelm, who added a huge quadrangular open-plan hall, shed roofs and dispersing ceiling lights for changing exhibitions.

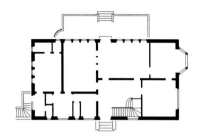

KOPP VILLA

REALISED 1910–1911
PLANNER Paul Bonatz
ADDRESS Gellertstrasse 6
ACCESS Restricted

Around the turn of the last century downtown Stuttgart was very densely populated and polluted by the manufacturing industry. Those who could, therefore built on the hillsides around the city. Killesberg, Bopser, Wagner-höhe and Gänsheide were the most attractive sites for the villas of wealthy people like Robert Bosch, for whom Jacob Früh and Carl Heim built a villa in the style of romantic-classicism with an asymmetrical plan and a slender tower in 1911. In the same year Paul Bonatz finished his paradigm-shifting Kopp Villa: the cuboid house with hipped roof, sparse ornamentation and freely associated classical elements is a typical example of the reform-architecture of Theodor Fischer and his pupil Bonatz. While the entrance door is located in the middle of the façade the windows are organised asymmetrically, reflecting the layout inside the house. The entrance hall houses the stairs and leads into the living room, which opens onto the garden. Contrary to this axial scheme, the other spaces are asymmetrical. Bonatz used this design for his own house on Gellerstrasse 8, which was re-built and altered by Paul Darius after WW II.

NEARBY Kanonenhäusle (1702/1863, Gellerstrasse 12), Wagenburg Grammar School (1914, Martin Elsaesser, Wagenburgstrasse 30)

BOSCH FACTORY BUILDINGS
Bosch Fabriksbauten

Hoppenlau Cemetery

Bosch property in 1937

REALISED 1910–1912/1997–2001
PLANNER Carl Heim, Jakob Früh/ARGE Ostertag & Vornholt, Heinle, Wischer und Partner
ADDRESS Breitscheidstrasse 4–8
ACCESS Restricted

In 1901 Bosch moved its production to the area between Seidenstrasse, Rosenbergstrasse and Breitscheidstrasse, where the company commissioned several factory buildings, amongst others by the architects Carl Heim and Jakob Früh. Between 1910 and 1912 they realised three factory buildings aligned perpendicular to the Breitscheidstrasse. The buildings' supporting structure was made of concrete; the façades were the first to be realised in exposed concrete in Württemberg. Though not favoured by the local building authorities, concrete and a skeleton structure enabled revolutionary, flexible floor plans. For the façades of the five- to six-storey buildings a construction system of main and secondary beams (that was in line with the functional character of the design) and concrete (which was filled into a textured formwork and later shaped and ornamented by stonemasons) was used. During WW II the area was mostly destroyed, then redeveloped, but its future became uncertain. When Bosch left it in 1970, the state Baden-Württemberg purchased the site for office space. In the early 1990s an architects' consortium started a comprehensive conversion of the Bosch areal.

NEARBY Old Riding Arena (1888, Robert Reinhardt, Forststrasse 2a), St Fidelis (1925, Clemens Hummels, Seidenstrasse 41), Russian Orthodox St Nicholas Cathedral (1895, Eisenlohr & Weigle, Kornbergstrasse 20b)

GYM AND FESTIVAL HALL FEUERBACH

Turn- und Festspielhalle Feuerbach

REALISED 1912
PLANNER Bonatz & Scholer
ADDRESS Kärntner Strasse 46–50
ACCESS Restricted

The festival hall is part of an educational ensemble planned by Paul Bonatz and Friedrich Eugen Scholer containing the hall itself, its surrounding park, the festival place with two small entrance buildings and the Leibniz School (1912). The hall was built as a gym for the pupils as well as space for exhibitions and cultural events. The axial system of the whole complex gives the site the feeling of a castle complex with the school building as castle and the festival hall as pleasure house. The main entrance is located in the south and leads the visitor across the large festival place towards the festival hall. A wide, flat staircase allows access to the elevated hall. The edifice consists of the two-storey core with a dragged hip roof and the festival hall. It is surrounded by a lower annex with a roof terrace that is connected to a gallery on the inside. The plastered brick façade is plain, with very little ornamentation. It is sectioned by white, wooden doors and windows. The interior was ornamented with wooden elements but after structural changes in 1978–1982 only the wide, coloured wooden ceiling in the gym remains.

NEARBY ECA estate 'Am Heimberg' (1953, Gero Karrer, Max Hausschild, Wiener Strasse 203–253)

011

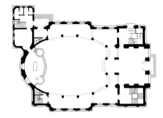

GAISBURG PARISH CHURCH
Gaisburger Stadtpfarrkirche

REALISED 1912–1913
PLANNER Martin Elsaesser
ADDRESS Faberstrasse 16
ACCESS Open to the public

Built in 1912–1913 by architect Martin Elsaesser in Stuttgart-Gaisburg, this protestant church marks a new style of sacred buildings at the beginning of the 20th century. Rectangular in shape and sitting on a hill, its soaring tower with tent roof over the main entrance turned it into a new landmark. In line with the classic form of the façade and baroque and renaissance elements like pilasters, flutes and mouldings, the main portal presents a tri-axial, superimposed portico. The high, adjoining entrance hall has a gallery. However, the principal uniqueness of Gaisburg Parish Church lies in the nave's organisation. The floor plan with baroque elements is defined by a spatial oval, marked by 14 green columns and a circumferential gallery. This centralisation of interior space pioneered a new kind of sacred building and reflected the contemporary innovations in liturgy. Elsaesser used the new principles of addition, integration and intersection to create a new spatial perception. Also impressive are the frescos of the artist Käte Schaller-Härlin in the choir, which illustrate scenes from the Old and New Testament.

STATE ACADEMY OF ART AND DESIGN

Staatliche Akademie der Bildenden Künste

REALISED 1912–1913
PLANNER Bernhard Pankok, Eisenlohr & Pfennig
ADDRESS Am Weissenhof 1
ACCESS Open to the public

Founded in the 18th century, the Stuttgart Academy of Art is one of the oldest and largest in Germany. When it was united with the school of arts and crafts (Kunstgewerbeschule) in 1941, it moved to a collegiate building on Killesberg which was built by Ludwig Eisenlohr and Oscar Pfennig and decisively influenced by its director Bernd Pankok (1912–13). The massive symmetrical, cuboid building, entirely made of concrete frames, is placed along the street Am Kochenhof facing an extensive open area. The plain main façade shows three floors with eleven window-axes each and a closed attic containing teaching rooms and studios illuminated by skylights. As the elegant façade with its almost square windows is kept simple with a few decorative elements, the elevated central entrance with its frame of two-storey colossal half columns attracts all the attention. A rounded cornice constitutes the upper façade seal and is topped by a high-hipped roof, which contrasts with the flat roofs of the other neighbouring younger college premises Neubau 1 (1968) and Neubau 2 (1994). The building was destroyed in WW II and rebuilt more simply.

NEARBY Residential Home Augustinum (2009, wulf architekten, Oskar-Schlemmer-Strasse), Killesberghöhe (2013, Baumschlager Eberle, David Chipperfield Architects, KCAP Architects, Ortner & Ortner Baukunst, Am Höhenpark, Am Kochenhof, Stresemannstrasse)

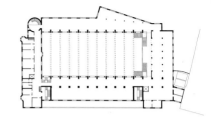

MARKET HALL
Markthalle

REALISED 1912–1914
PLANNER Martin Elsaesser
ADDRESS Dorotheenstrasse, Münzstrasse, Sporerstrasse
ACCESS Open to the public

The market hall is Stuttgart's urban, social and culinary heart. Located in the oldest part of town facing the Old Castle, it replaced the former 'Flower and Legumes Hall' that had been a diminutive copy of the Parisian Les Halles, but could not cater to the spatial and hygienic needs of the rapidly increasing population at the beginning of of the 20th century. To replace it, Elsaesser's design of a roofed but light-flooded market square surrounded by a representative arcade and gallery was chosen in 1910. He placed a four-storey, L-shaped volume vis-à-vis of the Old Castle and superimposed an arcade and two risalits to create a representative bourgeois façade. At the back, he adjusted the broad market hall, spanned by innovative concrete triple bearers with two glass levels developed by Wayss & Freytag. As the ground floor of the hall declines from west to east by half a storey, the rear tract is two storeys high, containing an interposed mezzanine with flats for the market staff. By using formal elements of the adjacent medieval neighbourhood, the architect linked the new enormous volume to the urban context at the core of the city.

NEARBY Old Castle (1578, Aberlin Tretsch, Blasius Berwart/later conversions, Schillerplatz 6), former Orphanage (1712, Philipp Joseph Jenisch, Johann Ulrich Heim/later conversions, Charlottenplatz 17)

MAIN STATION
Hauptbahnhof

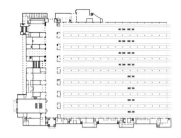

REALISED 1914–1928/since 2010
PLANNER Bonatz & Scholer/Ingenhoven
Architects with Frei Otto
ADDRESS Arnulf-Klett-Platz 2
ACCESS Open to the public

In 1910 Paul Bonatz and Friedrich Eugen Scholer won the competition to replace the old station at the former Schlossstrasse (today Bolzstrasse) built by Karl Etzel in the mid-19th century. Their 'umbilicus sueviae', the Swabian navel, is composed of several cuboid volumes. Two ticket halls at each end structure the main façade facing the city. Both halls emerge from the main body of the building, the 26-pillar colonnade, which bears a powerful attic, and are accessed through arched entrances resembling city gates. The 56 m high clock tower, recessed at the east elevation, correlates with the end of the Königstrasse. Hence, the main hall, that extends across the entire building, is raised above street level and the entrance halls are dominated by large stairways connecting the inside to the outside. Along the south hall high, juxtaposed arches grant access to the platforms. The station was designed as a reinforced concrete construction and then clad with shell limestone. Currently, the station is being converted to a subterranean transit station. In 1997 Ingenhoven Architects in cooperation with Frei Otto won the competition.

NEARBY Former Hindenburgbau (1928, Paul Schmohl, Georg Staehlin, Albert Eitel, Richard Bielenberg, Arnulf-Klett-Platz 1-3), Administration Building of Südwest Landesbank (1994, AP Plan, Versandstrasse)

1918–1933

During the interwar period, the inner city underwent very little structural change. With the opening of the new main station in 1928, the Arnulf-Klett-Platz in front of the station and the Lautenschlagerstrasse on the former trackbed were redeveloped and new buildings quickly sprung up (Hindenburgbau, Paul Schmohl, 1928; Oberpostdirektion, 1928). The Schocken department store of Erich Mendelsohn (1928) with its expressive forms (demolished in 1960) and the Tagblatt Tower as Stuttgart's first high-rise building set a new course for the inner city. At the market square, the department store Breuninger spread out with expansive new buildings (Eisenlohr & Pfennig, 1931).

However, the focus of the development lay on educational buildings as well as on housing development for the growing population of the state capital of Württemberg. As new construction areas were rare in the basin, building activity concentrated on the ridges and hillsides as well as in the suburbs. With the Postdörfle close to today's Heilbronner Strasse (Georg Morlok, 1872), the Ostheim colony (Gebhardt und Hengerer, 1896), plus the garden cities of Luginsland in Untertürkheim (1913) and Falterau in Degerloch (1914) Stuttgart already had a long tradition of housing developments.

The estates of the interwar period, like the Raitelsberg estate (1928), the Schönbühl estate (1930) or the Wallmer estate in Untertürkheim (1930) are characterised by terrace houses. Traditional building types were used at the Viergiebelweg colony planned by Döcker and Keuerleber (1922–1926).

The simultaneity of buildings of a rather modern style and those designed in a traditional way can also be found in single-family houses and in educational buildings: the tradition of the school buildings of Fischer, Bonatz, and Elsaesser was continued, but with the Raitelsberg school (Alfred Daiber, 1929) and the Städtische Handelsschule (Gerhard Graubner, 1929) modern design schemes were introduced into the educational building sector. Regarding the single family and apartment building development, at least since the completion of the Weissenhof estate, traditional and modern types of construction are opposing each other. The single-family houses by Bonatz and Schmitthenner continue the reform architecture of the pre-war period. The Roser Country House (1921), the Porsche House (1924) and Bonatz's own house (1922) as well as the villas Rassbach (1925) and Roser (1926) by Paul Schmitthenner show traditional roof shapes and materials. In strong contrast to this were the cubic buildings of the Weissenhof estate.

015

ROSER VILLA

REALISED 1925–1926

PLANNER Paul Schmitthenner

ADDRESS Feuerbacher Weg 51

ACCESS None

Several years after Paul Bonatz' design of a country house for the industrialist family Roser, Paul Schmitthenner was assigned to construct their new representative, upper class residence in the conservative 'Heimatstil'. The cubic, two-storey brick building, plastered with slurry finery represents a typical example of Schmitthenner houses in the style of the 'Stuttgart School'. The plinth is made of quarry stone. The high rising hipped roof is covered with plain tiles. Horizontal window axes and a particular hierarchy of window sizes and forms lend regularity to the two main façades on the north and south. Reflecting this symmetry, the ground floor is clearly structured with a centrally placed hall, leading to the surrounding rooms. While the floor and the jamb in the central hall are made of red sandstone, the living rooms have a wooden floor. The block-like closeness as well as the reduced design and decor and the axis-symmetric pattern in elevation and floor plan are characteristic of Schmitthenner's work. Along with his design of Rassbach Villa, the Roser Villa soon advanced to a design prototype for a traditional German house.

NEARBY House Porsche (1924, Paul Bonatz, Feuerbacher Weg 48–50), Roser Country House (1921, Bonatz & Scholer, Am Bismarckturm 58), Diplomat Estate (1956, Werner Gabriel, Albrecht-Dürer-Weg 15–21)

016

EIERNEST ESTATE
Siedlung Eiernest

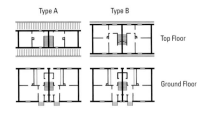

Type A Type B

Top Floor

Ground Floor

REALISED 1926–1927
PLANNER Stuttgart Building Construction Office
ADDRESS Eierstrasse, Liebigstrasse, Schreiberstrasse
ACCESS Restricted

This residential development was built for urban workers and employees to ease Stuttgart's housing shortage in 1925/26. Under the direction of the Stuttgart Building Construction Office the four hectare plot was developed and the affordable housing project with about 180 terrace houses for families was realised in just two years. As the street slopes gently, the houses were designed separately, their height correlating in proportion with the width of the street. The two-storey single family house was built as a lightweight construction. The wooden structure with its high double pitch roof appears to be traditional and simple. The wooden doors, windows and folding shutters order the façade, which was plastered in pale colours. Each floor is approximately 45 m². The first floor originally consisted of two rooms, a kitchen and a bathroom, the second floor of at least two bedrooms and an attic space. The design of the residential streets, front gardens and 'village' junctions goes back to the English garden city movement, which influenced residential development of Germany.

NEARBY Marienkrankenhaus Extension (1990, Franz Brümmendorf, Otmar Müller, Helmut Murr, Rolf Reichmann, Böheimstrasse 37)

017

MITTNACHT BUILDING
Mittnachtbau

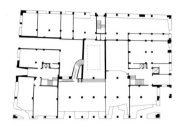

REALISED 1926–1928
PLANNER Eisenlohr & Pfennig
ADDRESS Königstrasse 46
ACCESS Restricted

The office building, named after Hermann Freiherr von Mittnacht (1825–1909), former prime minister of Württemberg, goes back to the design of Eisenlohr and Pfennig (1922) to highlight the main transportation artery to the new central station. It quickly became a new landmark of Stuttgart and marked the start of the modern movement. The cubic building and its prominent tower (communicating with the train station) was built of reinforced concrete and clad with travertine stone. Window sills resembling the ribbons of a box subdivide the seven-storey façade of the building's main volume along the Königstrasse. The floor division is perfectly proportional: the first and second floors are higher than the subsequent floors above, while the top floor with its cornice is the lowest. The building was originally designed as an office building to meet the need for more office space in 1927–1929. The first and second floor housed shops and there was also a café with roof terrace on the top floor of the tower. The building was damaged during WW II. The glazed oriel of the second floor corner was added during restoration in 1953.

NEARBY Pedestrian zone Schulstrasse (1958, Stuttgart Building Construction Office, Schulstrasse), Department Store Galeria Kaufhof (1960–1961, Egon Eiermann, Eberhardstrasse 28)

018

WEISSENHOF ESTATE
Weissenhofsiedlung

REALISED 1927

PLANNER Mies van der Rohe (urban masterplan, art direction and houses 1–4), Jacobus Johannes Pieter Oud (5–9), Victor Bourgeois (10), Adolf Gustav Schneck (11, 12), Le Corbusier & Pierre Jeanneret (13, 14–15), Walter Gropius (16, 17), Ludwig Hilberseimer (18), Bruno Taut (19), Hans Poelzig (20), Richard Döcker (21, 22), Max Taut (23, 24), Adolf Rading (25), Josef Frank (26, 27), Mart Stam (28–30), Peter Behrens (31–32), Hans Scharoun (33).

ADDRESS Am Weissenhof, Bruckmannweg, Friedrich-Ebert-Strasse, Hölzel-weg, Pankokweg, Rathenaustrasse

ACCESS Restricted

In summer 1927 about 500,000 people visited the experimental exhibition 'Building the House' on the Killesberg. Thirty-three terrace and detached houses as well as apartment buildings containing sixty-three dwellings constructed by seventeen architects were opened for visitors. The designs were based on a comprehensive model-housing programme for the modern urbanite, combining architecture and an interior design that was created by a further fifty-five architects and artists. Demonstrating an architectural revolution using cubic forms, flat roofs, new building techniques and materials, the houses were no longer objects of representation but something to be used. A minimum of form should guarantee a maximum of freedom. A new layout arrangement supported the life of the independent employed woman and implemented hygienic and airy living standards.

Flanked by the so-called 'Experimental Field' the Weissenhof estate was the culmination of the comprehensive German Werkbund's exhibition 'The Dwelling'. The 'International Plan and Model Exhibition of New Architecture'

Preserved Houses
Destroyed Houses

was shown in the castle gardens, the topic of the 'Furnishing of the House' was located in the Craft Halls in the city park. The project development started in 1925, initiated by Gustav Stotz, founder of the Werkbund's Württemberg section, and its chairman Peter Bruckmann. The city of Stuttgart provided the plot and a construction loan. Ludwig Mies van der Rohe was commissioned to develop an urban concept and to take responsibility for the art direction. Ten different lists of architects' names were discussed until the end of 1926. The finalists came from Germany, the Netherlands, Belgium, France and Austria, only two Stuttgart architects were involved (Richard Döcker and Adolf Schneck).

The realised houses influenced the Werkbund estates in Wrocław, Brno, Vienna, Prague and Zurich. However, when realised, the houses were too expensive for workers' families, thus failing on the social side. Furthermore, only a few architects used new materials and construction methods, such as for instance as Walter Gropius, who chose prefabricated steel frameworks. Bonatz and Schmitthenner were scathing of the exhibition straight away, but it was not until after 1933 that the criticism grew louder. In WW II and the post-war area ten houses were lost, nine houses were re-erected. The plot of house 21 has been left empty; it currently hosts the temporary experimental house B10 by Werner Sobek. In 2006 Le Corbusier's semi-detached house became a museum and together with the adjoining single-family house became a UNESCO world heritage site in summer 2016.

NEARBY Residential Home Augustinum (2009, wulf architekten, Oskar-Schlemmer-Strasse 5)

019

TAGBLATT TOWER
Tagblattturm

REALISED 1927–1928
PLANNER Ernst Otto Oßwald
ADDRESS Eberhardstrasse 61
ACCESS Restricted

The Tagblatt Tower is named after its client and first owner: the Stuttgart Neues Tagblatt newspaper. Though some famous names like Paul Bonatz and other representatives of the 'Stuttgart School' participated in the competition, it was the design of the unknown architect Oßwald that was finally chosen. The tower is built in the International Style and displays an exposed concrete façade with a bush-hammered finish. Erected in just 1.5 years the 61 m high building with its eighteen storeys was the first high-rise building in the region of Stuttgart and the highest in whole of southern Germany. Several vertical cubic volumes of different heights were combined to form the tower, giving it a soft ending at the top. On two sides of the tower, the façade has modern ribbon windows. The old neon tube lights were applied to the façade to emphasise the form of the building. The floor plan is not completely rectangular which is characteristic of a modern building. On the upper floors it has an open floor plan with open space offices. The 13th storey was to become Oßwald's own architectural office.

NEARBY Department Store Galeria Kaufhof (1960–1961, Egon Eiermann, Eberhardstrasse 28)

020

FRIEDRICH-EBERT COURT
Friedrich-Ebert-Wohnhof

—

REALISED 1927–1929/1938
PLANNER Karl Beer/Paul Schmitthenner
ADDRESS Hölzelweg 2
ACCESS Restricted

—

Friedrich-Ebert Court was realised on behalf of the 'Bau- und Heimstätten-vereins Stuttgart' by Karl Beer 1927–1929. Though one of the most note-worthy examples of the modern movement in Stuttgart and pendant to the Weissenhof estate, it was modelled on the large, contemporary welfare housing projects realised in Vienna to counter the housing shortage in the 1920s. Named after the first democratically elected president of the German Reich, Friedrich Ebert, the complex is composed of three volumes, all rendered in white with red window sills: three five-storey residential wings, a high-rise apartment building (eight storeys) and a two-storey restaurant hall, the 'Schönblick'. Combined, they form an irregular four-winged complex around a central courtyard—a widely visible landmark of the Internation-al Style in Stuttgart. The staircase tower with its narrow, long-stretched window overreaches the vertical cubic structure. Typical for contemporary flat roof constructions, the top of the façade only has marginal openings in the form of slender window slots. The roofs are gently inclined gable roofs, hidden behind an elevated parapet.

—

NEARBY Residential Home Augustinum (2009, wulf architekten, Oskar-Schlemmer-Strasse 5)

—

021

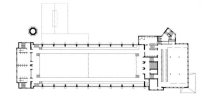

HESLACH PUBLIC BATHS
Stadtbad Heslach

REALISED 1927–1929
PLANNER Friedrich Fischle, Franz Cloos
ADDRESS Mörikestrasse 62
ACCESS Open to the public

At its opening in 1929 the public baths in Heslach were the biggest and most modern public bathhouse in Germany. Back then, the swimming hall's design, spatial arrangement and roof construction used sensational innovations for a breathtaking contemporary design. The four-storey, cubic building was built of reinforced concrete, but clad with red bricks. The façade of the entrance building at the north side has square lattice windows, and higher rectangular windows on the ground floor. The skeleton construction of the swimming hall is made visible by the pillars on the outside façade. They bear the large parabolic reinforced concrete bows spanning the swimming pool and large glass intercolumniations used to ventilate the hall. Inside, the visible bows support the stepped flat roof and create a dynamic impression that contrasts with the plain façade. From a functional perspective the architects reorganised the bathing experience: they located the changing rooms and massage parlours on the lower floor and invented a barefoot passage to the enlarged swimming pool in the upper storey that could be separated by gender.

NEARBY Schickhart Sports Hall (1983, AP Plan, Schickhardtstrasse 26), Generational House Heslach (2001, Drei Architekten Haag, Haffner, Strohecker, Gebrüder-Schmid-Weg 13)

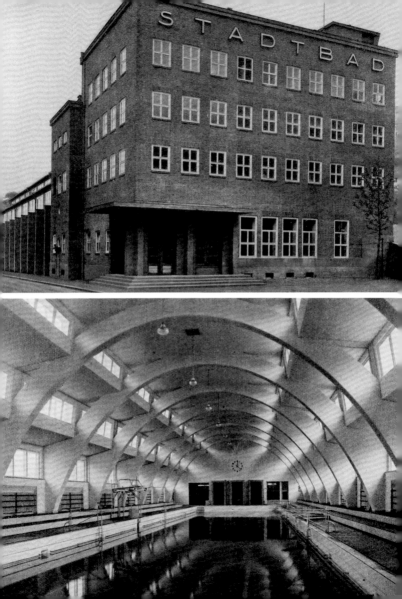

BAD CANNSTATT BARRAGE
Staustufe Bad Cannstatt

—

REALISED 1927–1930
PLANNER Paul Bonatz
ADDRESS König-Karls-Brücke
ACCESS Restricted

In 1920 a comprehensive programme was adopted to make the river Neckar navigable and to do away with towing and chain shipping. For this twenty-seven barrages and retaining weirs were to be constructed in two phases. Most of these barrages between Stuttgart and Mannheim were designed by Paul Bonatz, who was commissioned as consulting architect in 1927. Bonatz kept his designs for these functional buildings serving technical needs very simple and clear. In general, they have four piers and inserted, movable barrage gates, chamber locks and a generator house to save energy. The piers have a block shape: facing upriver the cubic frontage slows the arriving water, facing downriver the piers taper and thus give the water new momentum. Under the thin roof, ribbon windows trace the outline of the parabolic layout. In some cases Bonatz emphasised this storey with bricks to create a contrast to the ensemble's concrete surface. The Bad Cannstatt Barrage with its three piers and lock, which was built in the 1950s, is the first of its kind that functioned simultaneously as a weir and power plant (on the south weir).

—

NEARBY Rosenstein Castle Museum (1829, Giovanni Salucci, Rosensteinpark), Leuze Spa (1954, Hellmut Weber, Otto Herbert Hajek, Am Leuzebad 1–6)

023

FORMER TELEGRAPH CONSTRUCTION OFFICE
Ehemaliges Telegrafenbauamt

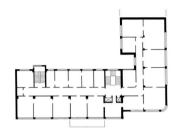

REALISED 1929–1930

PLANNER Otto Oßwald

ADDRESS Neckarstrasse 145

ACCESS Restricted

The building was constructed for the former Reichspost according to the design of the post office building surveyor Otto Oßwald. The shape of its two plain cuboids follows the progressive forms of the International Style. The larger seven-storey elongated structure orientated to Neckarstrasse has ribbon windows for each storey, continuing at the corner that are underlined by cantilevered mouldings and only interrupted by the load-bearing quadrangular pillars. A double thoroughfare leads to the courtyard behind. The smaller four-storey volume is arranged orthogonaly to the first, but has a rounded corner and houses the original main entrance. The ensemble was supposed to be the prelude of a technical building of 140 m in length, which was never realised. From 1945 to 1976 the building was the headquarters of the Süddeutscher Rundfunk broadcasting company. Because of a space shortage in 1954 a large extension was added at the west-facing side along the street. Today, the former exposed concrete façades are rendered. Since 1977 the Stuttgart Prosecution Service has resided in the complex.

NEARBY Interior Ministry (2013, Volker Staab Architekten, Willy-Brandt-Strasse 41)

024

HOHENSTEIN SCHOOL
Hohenstein-Schule

—

REALISED 1929–1930
PLANNER Paul Schmitthenner
ADDRESS Hohensteinstrasse 25
ACCESS None

—

The Hohenstein School was to serve the needs of the expanding suburb of Zuffenhausen. The building was to house a vocational school, a business school, a home economics school as well as a primary and secondary school. In the competition of 1927 Paul Schmitthenner provided a three-winged and angled complex with a flat-hipped roof flanking the plot's borders with short side wings. The longer middle wings expand from north to south separating the outer spaces into a recreational and an exercise area. Only a two-storey gatehouse with a high-hipped roof at the site's northeast corner acts as a counterpoint to the huge four-storey volume. Tower-like block aprons mark the staircases at the building's ends. While the north and middle wings house classrooms, the southern wing with its higher windows and an axis-symmetric double flight stair contains a gym. Aligned quadrangular windows give the reduced brick façade its rhythm. Clear, reduced forms characterise the building's appearance, but its details reveal the fusion of modern and traditional elements that is the hallmark of the architectural doctrines of the 'Stuttgart School'.

—

NEARBY Senior Housing Estate St Antonius (2001, LRO Lederer Ragnarsdóttir Oei, Besigheimer Strasse 19)

—

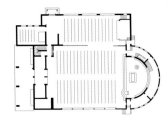

CRUCIFORM CHURCH (NEW CHURCH)
Kreuzkirche (Neue Kirche)

REALISED 1929–1930
PLANNER Paul Trüdinger and Hans Volkart
ADDRESS Amstätterstrasse 25
ACCESS Open to the public

At the end of the 1920s, shortly after the opening of internationaly acclaimed Weissenhof estate, the New Church was a contemporary design solution to cater for the growing Christian community of the industrial suburb Hedelfingen. After a long selection process the parish chose the design containing variable hall sizes by architects Trüdinger and Volkart due to its flexibility. The realised steel-frame sacral building consists of two volumes, a 46 m long and 30 m wide double height parallelepiped space corresponding to the nave, sanctuary and community hall of the church, and the five-storey bell tower added to the western side of the building. The wide column-free structure permits thin walls, a flat roof and the church's nave to be extended into the community hall. As to light, a slender coloured lead window band makes the roof float and vertical rectangular window slots illuminate the semi-circled apsis at the end of the nave. The crucifix on the top of the bell tower gave the church its new name in 1980, as the name New Church had become obsolete after fifty years of existence.

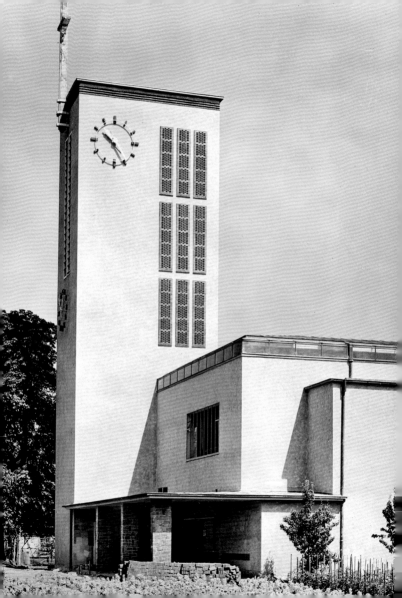

026

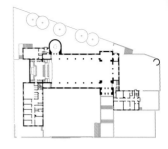

ST GEORG CHURCH
Kirche St Georg

—

REALISED 1929–1930
PLANNER Hugo Schlösser
ADDRESS Heilbronner Strasse 135
ACCESS Open to the public

Designed by Hugo Schlösser in 1929/30, the catholic church of St Georg represents one of Stuttgart's most important sacred buildings of its time—modern, modest, yet, monumental. A parish hall on the left and the rectory on the right, the monumental complex rests parallel to the slope of the Killesberg. In front of it a parvis opens up, which is reached by broad stairs. In contrast to the cuboid, horizontally arranged volumes, the powerful, 40 m spire is the only vertical and holds the main entrance. At its top, horizontal lamellar cornices accentuate the vertical acoustic openings. The church itself is a conventional three-nave basilica in which the side naves have been reduced to alleyways with barrel-vaults. The main nave has a flat ceiling. Simplicity and artlessness radiate through the clearly structured floor plan, the building's interior design and the exterior red-violet clinker cladding of the steel-reinforced structure. Inspired by the northern German expressionism of the early 20th century the white interior with its sterile and simultaneously ceremonial expression is reminiscent of early Christian churches.

—

NEARBY School Complex North (1982, Refurbishment 2015, wulf architekten, Heilbronner Strasse 153–159)

—

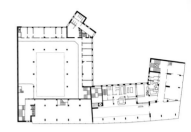

027

ZEPPELIN BUILDING
Zeppelinbau

—

REALISED 1929–1931
PLANNER Bonatz & Scholer
ADDRESS Lautenschlagerstrasse 2
ACCESS Restricted

The seven-storey building of Paul Bonatz and Friedrich Eugen Scholer consists of one parallelepiped reinforced concrete volume, whose façade is subdivided in four horizontal layers. A row of pillars on both sides of the double-height ground floor accessible from the Lautenschlagerstrasse and Arnulf-Klett-Platz permits an uncluttered space, behind which the main entrance, restaurants and shops line up. As the still original façade is non-load-bearing, a continuous band of windows stretches along the second floor making the structure appear light. On the next three floors, windows at regular intervals structure the façade; the grid changes on the last two floors, when the façade recedes on the longer side to the Lautenschlager-strasse and the intervals of the windows become wider. A flat roof ends the building—one indicator of the modern movement. Located opposite the Main Station the building has mostly been used as hotel. In 1931 it contained the Girozentrale, the state bank of that time and the hotel 'Graf Zeppelin', from 1957 onwards the luxury hotel Steigenberger for which the extension of the Zeppelinbau was finished in 1971.

—

NEARBY Former Hindenburgbau (1928, Paul Schmohl, Georg Staehlin, Albert Eitel, Richard Bielenberg, Arnulf-Klett-Platz 1-3), Administration Building of Südwest Landesbank (1994, AP Plan, Versandstrasse)

—

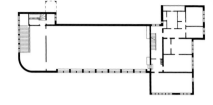

BRENZ CHURCH
Brenzkirche

REALISED 1932–1933
PLANNER Alfred Daiber
ADDRESS Am Kochenhof 7
ACCESS Open to the public

At the beginning of the 1930s Alfred Daiber designed the Brenz Chuch as a very modern and modest two-storey church reflecting the aesthetic philosophy of the International Style. Its main body consists of one cuboid to which two smaller ones were added on the longer sides. The architect located the great hall on the upper floor and included a parish hall, a kindergarten and flats below. One edge of the façade was rounded following the street course. The building had large windows (including ribbon ones) and an open skeleton construction for a bell tower. Carried by two very slim pillars, it rested on the flat roof. On completion in 1933 the National Socialists mocked it as a cigar-factory or a 'soul-silo'. In 1939 it was suddenly decided to reconstruct the Brenz Church for the Reichsgartenschau (national garden expo) as its style was not in accordance with Nazi ideology. The round became cornered, the tall glass surfaces were replaced by crown glass, the roof was gabled and the open bell tower was closed. Thus transformed, the building is almost unrecognisable today. Only the staircase hints at the originally rounded façade.

NEARBY Killesberghöhe (2013, Baumschlager Eberle, David Chipperfield Architects, KCAP Architects, Ortner & Ortner Baukunst, Am Höhenpark, Am Kochenhof, Stresemannstrasse)

At the opening of the building exhibition 'German Wood for House Building and Dwelling' and the accompanying Kochenhof estate swastika flags were already flown above the entrance. The settlement, planned by Paul Schmitthenner and urban planner Heinz Wetzel, presented traditional forms of construction combined with modern serial constructions and showed a deliberate contrast to the international modernity of the Weissenhof estate, which had already been branded a 'Bolshevik blot'.

Planning for the inner city under the Nazis suggested a traffic ring with large axes, a freeway-like street through the castle gardens and squares for military deployment. The relocation of the station to the Neckar and the development of the Uhlandshöhe, the Rosensteinpark and the Karlshöhe with huge buildings for the Nazi party were considered. Even more specific were the plans for the construction of a Gauforum near the town hall. In fact, little was realised. Though a monstrous honorary hall for the 'Reichsnährstand' and an amusement area were built for the Reichsgartenschau (national garden expo) on the Killesberg in 1939, the only other large buildings to be completed were Adolf Hitler's Kampfbahn (now the Mercedes-Benz Arena), enclosed by mighty colonnades and designed by Bonatz & Scholer (1933/35), and the airport by Ernst Sagebiel

(1938) in Leinfelden-Echterdingen. Another infrastructure project was the highway from Karlsruhe via Stuttgart to Munich, an immediate answer to the steadily growing traffic, which also had to be increasingly taken into consideration in the inner city.

Concerning infrastructure development and the local construction statutes, the planning guidelines of the Nazi period (laid down in 1935 and prescribing densely built areas in the inner city and areas with low density along the hillsides) remained effective in the post-war period. Silent witnesses to the Nazi building policy are 14 travertine columns across the street from the power station in Münster, which were originally intended for a large building in Berlin. The most significant role in Stuttgart's further urban history was played by the Allied forces, bombing the city and destroying more than half of the city. The medieval layout of Stuttgart, which mostly consisted of half-timbered buildings, burned down almost completely. Most of the massive building constructions of the inner city were also razed to the ground. After the unconditional surrender of the German Reich on May 1, 1945, Stuttgart presented itself to the urban planners and architects of reconstruction like a tabula rasa.

KOCHENHOF ESTATE
Kochenhofsiedlung

REALISED 1933

PLANNER Paul Schmitthenner (urban masterplan and houses 1, 2, 3), Bonatz & Scholer (4), Ernst Schwaderer (5), Paul Heim (6), Hermann Gabler (7), Hans Volkart (8), Gerhard Graubner (9), Richard Weber (10), Eugen Kiemle und Paul Weber (11), Albert und Hans Eitel (12), Alfred Kircherer (13), Eduard Krüger (14), Otto Köbele (15), Eisenlohr & Pfennig (16), Hellmut Weber (17), Walter Körte (18), Ernst Wagner (19), Ernst Leitner (20), Werner Pilzecker (21), Hans Mayer (22), Erhard Rommel und Erich Wiemken (23), Wilhelm Tiedje (24), Karl Gonser (25)

ADDRESS Carlos-Grethe-Weg, Hermann-Pleuer-Strasse, Kalckreuthweg, Otto-Reiniger-Strasse

ACCESS Restricted

The exhibition 'Deutsches Holz für Hausbau und Wohnung' (German Wood for House Building and Dwelling) of 1933 presented 25 single and multi-dwellings topped by saddle roofs and based on timber construction for all parts of the building (truss, back filling method or panel system) that was plastered, boarded or painted. The aim was to support the timber industry. The initial impulse for the Kochenhof estate was given by Paul Schmitt-henner, who, supported by his colleagues Heinz Wetzel and Paul Bonatz, drew up the master plan. The selected 23 architects or representatives of architectural offices had all been professors or former students of the Technical University Stuttgart and followers of the 'Stuttgart School'. This branch of the modern movement sought for innovations which respected traditional and regional styles while perceiving themselves as a counter movement to the cubic language of architects like Ludwig Mies van der Rohe, etc.

Therefore, the Kochenhof estate was communicated as a counter model to the Weissenhof estate. The planning process of the Weissenhof estate as well as the flat roof promoted by it, provoked the criticism of the most renowned regional architects Schmitthenner and Bonatz. Schmitthenner had tried to implement a second exhibition estate in Stuttgart which was in line with the doctrine of 'Stuttgart School' since 1927, but failed twice. Independently of Schmitthenner's ambitions, in 1932 Richard Döcker, former assistant of Bonatz and one of only two Stuttgart architects represented on the Weissenhof estate, was chosen to lead the second experimental settlement of the German Werkbund in Stuttgart on the site of today's Kochenhof estate involving nineteen architects.

In 1933, shortly after the beginning of the Third Reich, Schmitthenner intervened and the Werkbund's project was cancelled. Instead, Schmitthenner was commissioned to create a new urban layout with the Kochenhof estate. When this exhibition was opened in September 1933, swastika flags flanked the path to the wooden entrance pavilion with a shed roof positioned at the intersection of Am Kochenhof and Kalkreuthweg. Despite the fact that the estate was used for Nazi propaganda and in spite of the traditional appearance of the saddle roofs and punctuated façades, all houses present modern solutions like rectangular-shaped layouts offering skilful spatial savings and sophisticated functional ideas like the location of kitchen, the introduction of granny annexes, overlapping maisonettes, etc.

NEARBY 'Die Milchbar' (1950, Rolf Gutbrod, Höhenpark Killesberg)

030

FORMER SALES OFFICE OF BOSCH AG

Ehemaliges Verkaufsbüro der Bosch AG

REALISED 1933–1935
PLANNER Hans Hertlein
ADDRESS Seidenstrasse 36
ACCESS Restricted

The former sales office of Bosch AG is located at the edge of the 'Bosch Areal' at the crossroads of Seidenstrasse and Rosenbergstrasse. This six-storey, L-shaped building was built of reinforced concrete and is characterised by a big rounded corner at the crossroads, where the customer entrance is. Its uppermost floor is set back on Seidenstrasse and Rosenbergstrasse. Above the ground floor ribbon windows divide the red brick façade horizontally. The ground floor itself is arranged vertically to make the load-bearing system visible. Besides the sales office the building also contained offices for administration, store rooms and workshops. In the inner courtyard was a large single-storey factory hall with a saw-tooth roof. Inside, it is open plan; staircases, lifts, lavatories and cloakrooms were located in two cuboids that are orientated to the inner courtyard at the building's front sides. As the windows should allow in as much light as possible, the window posts have a slim design and the window frames reach up to the ceilings. Since 1970 the building has accommodated various institutes of Stuttgart University.

NEARBY Old Riding Arena (1888, Robert Reinhardt, Forststrasse 2a), St Fidelis (1925, Clemens Hummels, Seidenstrasse 41), Russian Orthodox St Nicholas Cathedral (1895, Eisenlohr & Weigle, Kornbergstrasse 20b)

031

VOGELSANG ESTATE
Vogelsangsiedlung

REALISED 1934–1939

PLANNER Albert und Hans Eitel (Botnanger Strasse 6–14), Paul Heim (Chamissostrasse 1–3), Eisenlohr & Pfennig (Chamissostrasse 6–8), Karl Gonser (Stirnbrandstrasse 3–5), Richard Döcker (Stirnbrandstrasse 8–10), Hans Volkart (Bebelstrasse 117)

ADDRESS Botnanger Strasse, Chamissostrasse, Stirnbrandstrasse, Bebelstrasse

ACCESS Restricted

The Vogelsang estate built between 1934 and 1939 in Stuttgart's hilly west is comprised of multi- and single-family homes. It was a project in line with the prevalent national socialist settlement politics and headed by Paul Bonatz and Paul Schmitthenner as artistic advisers. Eight different architects were offered a choice of thirty hillside lots on which to build. The multi-family homes are located along busy streets, while the single-family homes are in the quieter centre of the complex. Most of the single-family homes have private gardens either in the front or back, giving the complex a communal feeling while ensuring the separation of public and private life. Though timber-frame constructions, the buildings feature simple, white plaster façades with high-pitched gabled roofs and regularly spaced windows with small mullions and shutters. Many of the homes have small, two-storey extensions for entrances, garages, or sun rooms. In general, the houses share similar architectural features, creating a cohesive appearance. Since their construction though, renovations to certain properties have changed some of these features.

NEARBY Paul-Gerhardt-Hof (1953, Paul Heim, Rosenbergstrasse 194)

032

ST MARTIN CHURCH
Martinskirche

REALISED 1935–1937
PLANNER Karl Gonser
ADDRESS Eckartstrasse 2
ACCESS Restricted

Built in 1887 the original protestant St Martin Church close to the Prague Cemetery was a church for workers in the north of Stuttgart. As their numbers grew in the 1920s, Karl Gonser was commissioned to design a church for up to 1,000 people. Its exterior offers a simple gabled roof, interrupted on the south side by a four-storey bell tower above the main entrance. The tightly-jointed, smooth sandstone of the façade, produces a refined and simple aesthetic. The exterior mirrors the interior: the nave has a classic layout with an open gable roof that rises above the altar in the centre of the northern wall. On the east side, evenly-spaced, rectangular stained-glass windows form a contrast to the glazed wall of the circulation corridor opposite, which links the interior to the public courtyard in the west. On the north side of this courtyard, perpendicular to the church building, is a low annex that accommodates offices, a kitchen, and a few meeting spaces. Privacy can be found in the small chapel, located just off the entrance. Seriously damaged during WW II, the church was reconstructed in a simpler design in 1950.

NEARBY Prague Cemetery (1872, Friedhofstrasse 44), Memorial 'Zeichen der Erinnerung' Nordbahnhof (Otto-Umfrid-Strasse)

1945–1975

Unlike in Munich the decision in Stuttgart was not to reconstruct the heavily destroyed historical city but to pursue a new beginning after the war. When Richard Döcker, a former Weissenhof site manager and architect, was appointed Director of the Central Office for the Construction of Stuttgart (ZAS), he called for radical change. The city's functions were relocated: the museums and exhibition buildings were gathered at the castle gardens, the formerly multifunctional city park was transformed into the university campus, the city centre (following the Athens Charter) became the business and administrative centre, while residential areas were established in the industry-free east and south of the city and in large new development areas such as Zuffenhausen or Möhringen (Fasanenhof).

In line with the new beginning, even well-preserved 19th century buildings were replaced by modern constructions. Up until 1961 discussions were held about the demolition of the New Castle. Finally, traffic matters were given top priority. The expansion of today's Konrad-Adenauer-Strasse and Theodor-Heuss-Strasse into city highways detached the city centre from the neighbouring districts. From east to west these two axes are connected by the Schillerstrasse, the Planie and the Paulinenstrasse.

Enormous infrastructure projects were realised in the case of the Charlottenplatz (1961), where two main roads and two subway lines intersect, and the Kleiner Schlossplatz (1968), to which the Kronprinzenpalais had to give way.

The ideal of the car-friendly city on a modulated city landscape with outstanding special buildings was realised in a very confined space. The Concert Hall, the buildings of the university city campus, the Hahn office tower, the Baden-Württembergische Bank at the Kleiner Schlossplatz (Rolf Gutbrod, 1968) and the Allianz-Versicherung next to the Karlshöhe (Harald Deilmann, 1974) characterise the cityscape and compete with the historical buildings. Because the old parcelling was preserved on the market square, the modern buildings with their grid-like façades and flat or shed roofs show a peculiar mixture of medieval narrowness and modern forms and colours. In 1971, the heavy-weight beton-brut building of the Breuninger department store (Rainer R. Czermak) pushed into the market square.

In contrast, the ease and openness of the 1950s can be felt in 'Die Milchbar' on the Killesberg by Rolf Gutbrod (1950) or in Windstoßer House by Max Bächer (1959). In terms of sheer quantity, the building structure of Stuttgart is still shaped by the reconstruction and buildings of the boom years.

033

LOBA HOUSE
LOBA Haus

Ground floor

Upper floor

REALISED 1949–1950
PLANNER Rolf Gutbrod
ADDRESS Charlottenstrasse 29
ACCESS Restricted

The LOBA House is Stuttgart's first modern post-war office building with a curtain wall. Designed as the new headquarters of Süddeutsche Holzberufsgenossenschaft by Rolf Gutbrod, it is located in the south of downtown Stuttgart near Charlottenplatz and marks the corner of Charlottenstrasse and Blumenstrasse. The shape of the site determines the layout of the building: a V-shaped volume, consisting of two seven-storey wings meeting at an obtuse, cavetto-shaped angle. A circular staircase is positioned in the rear intersection connecting the different levels and leading up to the top floor. This staggered floor with its protruding roof over an expanded terrace is used as an apartment. The ground floor, offering space for two stores, is also set back and pivoted at the corner, thus creating a sheltered sidewalk for pedestrians. Between the top and ground floors there is office space behind the regular grid of the façade. Its homogeneous curtain-wall consists of slate-grey parapet elements, composed of corrugated fibre cement, aluminium windows and olive coloured vertical steel beams. Further contrast was provided by the red and white stripped awnings. Since 1952 an extension at Charlottenstrasse realised by Paul Stohrer supplements the LOBA House space.

NEARBY Post office and apartment house (1994, Wolfgang Stübler, Blumenstrasse 8)

034

HOUSE ENGLISCH
Haus Englisch

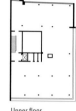

Ground floor   Upper floor

REALISED 1949, 1954–1955

PLANNER Paul Stohrer

ADDRESS Königstrasse 33

ACCESS Restricted

House Englisch, a redevelopment initially designed for the fashion store Englisch on Königstrasse, marks the corner to Neue Brücke leading down to the town hall. Having had to deal with the slope of the plot, the architect Paul Stohrer slid the lowest floor into the ground. The building was realised in two phases: the lower two floors built in 1949 housed shops on the ground floor at street level and a wine restaurant in the basement. From 1954 to 1955 five additional regular floors and a staggered top-floor were added, aligning the building with its surroundings. The floor plan goes back to the previous structure. Though not visible from outside, the floors of the current building therefore centre round a small courtyard. Except for this, the façade, consisting of non-load bearing fair-faced concrete frames, is subdivided into three horizontal zones: the fully glazed and transparent ground floor with the shops, the building's main volume, made up of the upper floors, and the staggered top floor. To give it a distinctive appearance, the parapet elements and closed façade elements are black while the other elements are white.

SPEISER OFFICE BUILDING
Geschäftshaus Speiser

REALISED 1950–1951
PLANNER Rolf Gutbier
ADDRESS Königstrasse 34
ACCESS Restricted

The Speiser office building is situated at the western corner of the Schloss-platz facing the main shopping street Königstrasse. Using the plot of the former department store 'Großer Bazar' it was designed as business house for the Speiser Store and the newspaper 'Stuttgarter Nachrichten'. The modern post-war solution of Rolf Gutbier displays an L-shaped volume, which blends into the perimeter development between Königstrasse and Kronprin-zenstrasse. On Königstrasse an eight-storey cuboid flanks the street, while the part facing the Kronprinzenstrasse has only six floors. The top staggered floor is covered by a signature cantilever roof. Its modern appearance is due to the steel frame construction and its non-load bearing façade on the upper floors consisting of parapets basing on corrugated aluminium windows with aluminium frames. The ground and first floor are glazed. Black I-beams section the building horizontally. Gutbier's draft for the Speiser office build-ing was influenced by the American architecture of the 1940s. Erected at the same time with Queen Olga Building, although very different, both structures are examples of post-war reconstruction.

NEARBY BW-Bank (1968, Rolf Gutbrod, Kleiner Schlossplatz 11)

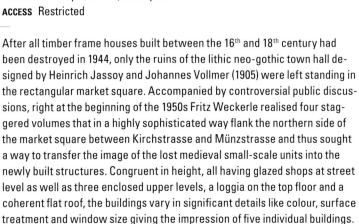

036

COMMERCIAL BUILDINGS AND TOWN HALL ON THE MARKET SQUARE
Geschäftshäuser und Rathaus am Marktplatz

REALISED 1950–1952; 1953–1956
PLANNER Fritz Weckerle; Hans Paul Schmohl und Paul Stohrer
ADDRESS Marktplatz 8–12; Marktplatz 1
ACCESS Restricted

After all timber frame houses built between the 16th and 18th century had been destroyed in 1944, only the ruins of the lithic neo-gothic town hall designed by Heinrich Jassoy and Johannes Vollmer (1905) were left standing in the rectangular market square. Accompanied by controversial public discussions, right at the beginning of the 1950s Fritz Weckerle realised four staggered volumes that in a highly sophisticated way flank the northern side of the market square between Kirchstrasse and Münzstrasse and thus sought a way to transfer the image of the lost medieval small-scale units into the newly built structures. Congruent in height, all having glazed shops at street level as well as three enclosed upper levels, a loggia on the top floor and a coherent flat roof, the buildings vary in significant details like colour, surface treatment and window size giving the impression of five individual buildings. Their restrained appearance and mixture of traditional and avant-garde elements reflect the search for the right form and expression of reconstruction in the historic environment after WW II.

Due to the prevailing negative attitude towards historicist legacy, the town hall was to be re-erected in a modern shape on the market square, while rear parts were to be refurbished and still present its historical form vocabulary. In their realised design Schmohl and Stohrer, who submitted two individual contributions to a competition in 1950, replaced the main façade with an extended cubic bar of six storeys.

Its new length causes an asymmetrical arrangement as the tower integrating the ancient supporting structure and the main entrance in its lower level moved from the centre. The strict grid of the town hall's façade towards the market place derives from the dimensions of the large, square windows. The tower and the entire new building were clad with bright shell limestone slabs from the Swabian Alb. Inside a paternoster connects the four floors.

For around 125 years the market square's history has been tightly connected to Breuninger on its north-east side. Unlike the buildings around it, the expansion of this building reflects the contemporary architectural tendencies at the time of expansion. The new design of Eisenlohr & Pfennig (1931), which displayed a purist shape of construction, distinctive storey brinks and a rounded corner, set a new trend. Destroyed in WW II it was reconstructed in altered shape and cladded. Remarkable is the post-war block-like addition of Rainer R. Czermak (1971) that, partly covered with timber, offers a hermetic exposed concrete façade to the market square. In 1988–1989 the Karls Passage was realised by Kammerer + Belz, Kucher und Partner. The newest voluminous extension is the Dorotheen-Quartier (2017) designed by Behnisch & Partner.

037

QUEEN OLGA BUILDING
Königin-Olga-Bau

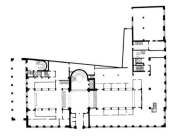

REALISED 1950–1954
PLANNER Paul Schmitthenner
ADDRESS Königstrasse 9
ACCESS Restricted

The Queen Olga Building is situated on the north end of the Schlossplatz at the corner of Königstrasse and Bolzstrasse and is a redevelopment for the Rhein-Main-Bank by Paul Schmitthenner as the original building of the same name was destroyed in WW II. The present office building completes the urban block of the Schlossplatz along Bolzstrasse between Königstrasse and Stauffenbergstrasse and provides an L-shaped volume with five floors. The latter are horizontally grouped in two zones that differ in appearance and material: the ground and first floors as well as the representative arcade along the Königstrasse and the main Schlossplatz entrance are clad with travertine, the upper floors with sandstone. The windows of the upper floors facing the Schlossplatz have characteristic shutters. On the buildings' top a floor containing an event room has been set back. With its cubic shape and high hip roof it appears like an individual house. Overall, however, the bank's monolithic architecture gives the building a solid appearance, which befits its use and makes it blend into the monumental buildings that surround the Schlossplatz.

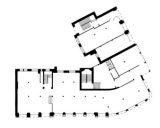

038

GERMAN HOUSE
Deutsches Haus

REALISED 1951–1952
PLANNER Heinz & Bodo Rasch
ADDRESS Tübinger Strasse 13–15
ACCESS Open to the public

The self-educated architect and former furniture designer Bodo Rasch aspired to achieve a utopian design of architecture and urban planning using the latest technological developments. In 1927/28 the Rasch brothers designed a residential building, which was hung from a mast using steel cables; as early as 1954 Bodo sketched a solar energy house. In the German House the architects tried to adjust mainstream post-war architectural design to fit the purpose of an office building. At the acute-angled site, where the straight Tübinger Strasse and curved Christoph Strasse meet, the Rasch brothers designed the remarkable building with a two-layered façade and flat roof topped by a staggered level. Along the streets they realised two conventional five-storey façades displaying a regular grid following the respective street lines, but at the corner, a second layer with six storeys was set back, thus breaking the rhythm. By subdividing the curved façade on Christoph Strasse with plastered parapet wall bands and ribbon windows, they recalled the aesthetics of the 1920s. On Tübinger Strasse an arcade is used for commercial purposes.

NEARBY Gerber Centre (2014, EDA Planungsgruppe GmbH/Architekturbüro Bernd Albers, Sophienstrasse 21)

039

UNIVERSITY CITY CAMPUS
Universitäts-Campus Stadtmitte

REALISED 1952–1964

PLANNER Max Kade House Max Kade-Haus, University Campus Cafeteria Universität Campus Stadtmitte Mensa I, both Wilhelm Tiedje and Ludwig H. Kresse, 1952–1953 / University Library Universitätsbibliothek Bibliothek, Hans Volkart, 1958–1961 / Collegiate Building KI and KII Kollegiengebäude KI und KII, Rolf Gutbier, Curt Siegel, Werner Gabriel, 1957–1965 / Institute for Manufacturing Engineering Institut für Fertigungstechnik, Hugo Berger (Hochschulbauleitung) 1960–1963 / 'Provisional' Auditorium Hörsaalprovisorium, Friedrich Wagner 1962.

ADDRESS Holzgartenstrasse, Kriegsbergstrasse, Breitscheidstrasse, Keplerstrasse

ACCESS Open to the public

After World War II the planners of the regional committee for the reconstruction of Stuttgart decided to convert the destroyed city park, located between Holzgartenstrasse and Hoppenlau Cemetery, into a University Campus. At that time the only buildings that had survived the war were the University of Applied Science (Hochschule für Technik, Josef von Egle, 1870) and a fragment of the former Technical University (Alexander von Tritschler, 1879, today the President's office). All the others are new constructions based on the urban concept of Richard Döcker and his aim to rebuild the park as an 'architectural landscape' consisting of several high-rises and flat buildings. The first of those was the 16-storey cubic student residence (Max Kade-House) by Tiedje and Kresse. They also built the adjacent canteen, in which a clever arrangement of rooms and a spiral stairs engenders a feeling of openness and flow. As opposed to this flux, the neighbouring Institute for Manufacturing Engineering is a suspended construction with five cantilevering floors around a tower-like lift shaft at its centre.

Max Kade House

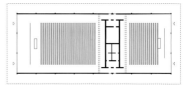

'Provisional' Auditorium

Collegiate Building KI

University Library

The expressionistic staggered shed roofed workshops of the institute form a contrast to this landmark. All three buildings open a dialogue with the two-storey, flat-roofed library with its integrated concrete pillars on its regular façade. Aluminium cladding along the verge of the roof emphasises the horizontal orientation of the building. Like an ancient temple it is positioned vis-à-vis the Linden Museum (Georg Eser, 1911). With its horizontal internal organisation the library offers substantial flexibility for large contiguous areas, open spaces and galleries that provide reading and shelf space. On its campus side the self-supporting construction of the auditorium provides a contrast. Built as a provisional lecture hall, it has a recoverable framework of a three-dimensional truss that spans longer distances.

The two cuboid high-rises KI and KII form the 'gate' to the city campus. Thought out by three professors, these collegiate buildings house, amongst others, the faculty of architecture. From the outside the buildings appear conventional; their inside layout, however, renders them unique. On the north side there are ten higher floors containing classrooms and workshops, on the south side fifteen lower floors for administration and offices. Two higher floors connect three lower floors with internal stairways that create a specific spatial quality. K I was built as a case study for fair-faced concrete and brick laying techniques as well as a didactic example of structural design.

NEARBY Linden Museum (1911, Georg Eser, Herdweg 1)

040

SILCHER SCHOOL
Silcherschule

REALISED 1952–1954
PLANNER Günter Wilhelm
ADDRESS Schwabbacher Strasse 25
ACCESS None

The school is located on a slope and was designed for the new district Rot in Stuttgart-Zuffenhausen. The architect Wilhelm was inspired by international school buildings, especially from Scandinavia, USA and Switzerland. As one of the first schools in Germany in line with this new type of school with open spaces, a lot of light and functional focused floor plans, the Silcher School met with acclaim throughout the German architecture community. The assemblage is organised around the main building, which contains all functional rooms, office and classrooms. The four buildings on the north side house the junior grades and a special-needs school and are adapted to the different requirements. The building in the south contains the vocational school with its own infrastructure. Most of the classrooms are lit from two sides by narrow window strips as well as by skylights and have cross ventilation to provide a healthy environment. A lightweight, partly covered steel skeleton stabilised by red bricks in the upper storeys and a concrete skeleton with concrete rib ceilings for the ground levels made building exceptionally cheap and quick.

NEARBY Senior Housing Estate St Antonius (2001, LRO Lederer Ragnarsdóttir Oei, Besigheimer Strasse 19)

041

U.S. GENERAL CONSULATE
US-Generalkonsulat

REALISED 1954
PLANNER SOM and Otto Apel
ADDRESS Urbanstrasse 7
ACCESS None

After WW II the United States built five new consulates across Germany, all designed by the American firm SOM. Inspired by Mies van der Rohe, these International Style buildings were an iconic expression of American culture. Built in cooperation with the Frankfurt architect Otto Apel, the three-storey building in Stuttgart has a simple cubic shape with a flat roof and a reinforced concrete frame. The façade has a horizontal orientation derived from the gridded aluminium-framed curtain wall. The upper portion of each storey contains a glazed component, while the lower half is comprised of a dark metal section. The programme of the building is divided into a typical consulate organisation with separate administrative and public areas. The ground floor is set back behind free-standing pillars in a slender, modern style that creates a rhythmic pattern. This elevation of the second floor gives the building a sense of lightness. The entrance hall is flanked by red granite slabs and tall windows, an arrangement which separates the building from the street. The lobby with a staircase and lift behind it is located in the foyer.

NEARBY Wilhelmspalais (1840, Giovanni Salucci, Conversion to City Library 1965, Wilhelm Tiedje, Conversion to City Museum 2018, LRO Lederer Ragnarsdóttir Oei, Konrad-Adenauer-Strasse 2)

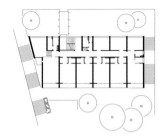

GEDOK HOUSE
GEDOK Haus

REALISED 1954
PLANNER Grit Bauer-Revellio
ADDRESS Hölderlinstrasse 17
ACCESS Restricted

The GEDOK community of German and Austrian female artists and art friends built its Stuttgart headquarters on the peak of a hillside property in 1954. Bauer Revellio's winning competition design emerged as an elongated five-storey structure, accommodating 27 one- and two-room apartments as well as 13 studios, an exhibition and a ballet hall. The studios are aligned along the upper street; opposite, the residential units face the southern sloping garden. The partitions forming loggias over the entire width of the room correspond to a residential unit, define each of the balconies and cabins. This cross-wall construction offers a unique design of transversely arranged load-bearing walls that exempts the external walls and the internal partitions from their static function. Altough the façade toward Hölderlinstrasse is plain, the structural framework of the transverse walls renders it special. Besides this, the emphasis is clearly on the staircase and entrance zone on the right side. The simplicity, the narrow, vertical strips of wall and plastering recall the architecture of the interwar period.

NEARBY Russian Orthodox St Nicholas Cathedral (1895, Eisenlohr & Weigle, Kornbergstrasse 20b)

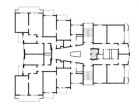

RAILWAY RESIDENTIAL TOWERS
Eisenbahner Wohnhochhäuser

REALISED 1954–1956
PLANNER Helmuth Conradi
ADDRESS Friedhofsstrasse 11, 25; Mönchstrasse 3, 5
ACCESS Restricted

The Railway Residential Towers are located between the Prague Cemetery and the former freight station. Commissioned by the Federal Railroad Construction Department and built to house federal railroad employees, the complex comprises four buildings, varying in height from eleven to fifteen storeys. Not only were the buildings the second skyscraper project in Stuttgart, they also stood out from other buildings at the time due to their dynamic shape and colourful façades. Their identical Y-shaped floorplan reminds the beholder of wings and flight, emphasised by their location on a hill. Made of concrete, the façades of each building feature ceramic plates, staggered balconies, and brightly coloured elements. The north side of each building has only a few windows and is painted in a different colour. The south sides with their integrated balconies are the narrowest points in the complex. Evenly spaced, exposed balconies mark the eastern and western façades. The apartments located on the top floors make use of the roof space, offering a unique view of the city. The core of the 'Y' contain circulation elements, lifts, and stairs.

NEARBY Skatepark (2009, MBA/S Matthias Bauer Associates, Canopy 2015, Herrmann + Bosch Architekten, Friedhofstrasse 30)

044

KING OF ENGLAND
König von England

REALISED 1954–1956
PLANNER Karl Gonser
ADDRESS Dorotheenstrasse 2
ACCESS Restricted

Surrounded by reconstructed buildings in Stuttgart city centre, King of England is a post-war construction. Used as office/retail space today, the original building served as a hotel and initially acquired its name from the marriage of Frederick I of Württemberg to the English princess Charlotte Auguste Mathilde. The architect of the new structure, Karl Gonser, used the market hall next door as context for the project by borrowing its hip roof and arcade passage. Using these elements, Gonser combined characteristics from the interwar style with 1950s design. The building is based on a rein-forced concrete skeletal structure. The gridded façade is clad with travertine tiles and embedded with deep cut, storey-high windows. The bottom third of each window contains frosted glass, while the upper two-thirds remain unfrosted; these, along with turquoise window frames, create a strong aes-thetic. The foyer stands in the corner, providing a staircase to the next levels. In 1960, an extension was created perpendicular to the original building. The slight curving nature of this new building forms an asymmetrical bay, which enlivens the simple façade.

045

TELEVISION TOWER
Fernsehturm

REALISED 1954–1956
PLANNER Fritz Leonhardt, Erwin Heinle
ADDRESS Jahnstrasse 120
ACCESS Open to the public

Standing on Hoher Bopser at an elevation of 483 m, the Television Tower rises 217 m into the sky. The tower was commissioned when television operation resumed after WW II, the site chosen for its height. Heinle served as artistic director, with Leonhardt responsible for the tower's design and structural analysis. Unlike the TV Tower's predecessors, it was made of reinforced concrete. In addition to being the first innovation in tower design since the Eiffel Tower, reinforced concrete was also more rigid and less costly than steel. With its elegant and simple appearance the tower offers a minimum of wind resistance. Its tapered shape starts at 11 m in diameter at the base and thins to 5 m. At 136 m the pin holds a four storey basket, which contains two storeys for restaurants and two for the transmission centre and kitchens, while the top serves as a multilevel observation deck. The interior design originated from Herta-Maria Witzemann. Lastly, a needle-shaped antenna tops the tower, making it rise to its final height. Though citizens of Stuttgart initially protested against the TV tower, it soon became an iconic landmark of the city and prototype for subsequent projects.

NEARBY House of the Woods (1997, Michael Jockers, Königssträssle 74)

046

CONCERT HALL
Liederhalle

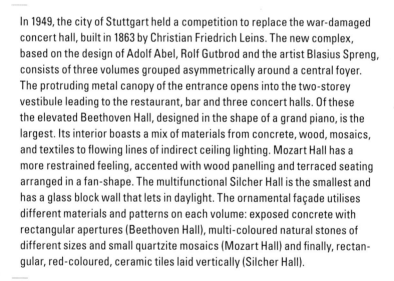

REALISED 1955–1956
PLANNER Adolf Abel, Rolf Gutbrod, Blasius Spreng
ADDRESS Berliner Platz 1
ACCESS Open to the public

In 1949, the city of Stuttgart held a competition to replace the war-damaged concert hall, built in 1863 by Christian Friedrich Leins. The new complex, based on the design of Adolf Abel, Rolf Gutbrod and the artist Blasius Spreng, consists of three volumes grouped asymmetrically around a central foyer. The protruding metal canopy of the entrance opens into the two-storey vestibule leading to the restaurant, bar and three concert halls. Of these the elevated Beethoven Hall, designed in the shape of a grand piano, is the largest. Its interior boasts a mix of materials from concrete, wood, mosaics, and textiles to flowing lines of indirect ceiling lighting. Mozart Hall has a more restrained feeling, accented with wood panelling and terraced seating arranged in a fan-shape. The multifunctional Silcher Hall is the smallest and has a glass block wall that lets in daylight. The ornamental façade utilises different materials and patterns on each volume: exposed concrete with rectangular apertures (Beethoven Hall), multi-coloured natural stones of different sizes and small quartzite mosaics (Mozart Hall) and finally, rectangular, red-coloured, ceramic tiles laid vertically (Silcher Hall).

NEARBY Congress Hall (1991, Wolfgang Henning, Berliner Platz 3)

SELF-SERVICE STORE
Selbstbedienungsladen

REALISED 1955–1956

PLANNER Eduard W. Hanow, Fritz Leonhardt

ADDRESS Gerokstrasse 12

ACCESS Open to the public

The small building on Gänsheide in Stuttgart east has a nationwide and historical significance for two different reasons. Its intention was to create an innovative design and to enable a new shopping experience. A concave, arched and plane load-bearing structure rests on two rows of twelve reinforced concrete columns, each creating an inward plate roof swinging upwards. This elegant and revolutionary shape was achieved by using a suspended roof structure with a lightweight concrete shell sprayed on a pre-stressed web of concrete cables. In 1955 it was the first suspended roof structure in Baden-Württemberg as well as the first use of a light concrete skin. The building was also the first supermarket opened in Stuttgart, entirely designed as a self-service shop. This uniqueness is reflected in the revolutionary design: no pillar was needed inside to support the roof structure. Hence the roof not only provided an advertising signal function, it also enabled an open plan layout for freely arranged shelving units like those already common in the United States.

NEARBY Wagenburg Grammar School (1914, Martin Elsaesser, Wagenburgstrasse 30)

048

'ROMEO AND JULIA' RESIDENTIAL TOWERS
Wohnhochhäuser 'Romeo und Julia'

REALISED 1955–1959
PLANNER Hans Scharoun, Wilhelm Frank
ADDRESS Schozacher Strasse 40, Schwabbacher Strasse 15
ACCESS None

The high-rise housing project in Zuffenhausen was Scharoun's first built post-war project, and the prototype for his later work. The roughly rectangular site is flanked by a busy road junction on three sides; this constraint determined the organisation of the privately funded project. The retail and residential complex is divided into two blocks, offering about 200 apartments. On the east, narrow end of the site is tall and thin Romeo, while the short and curved Julia with her twelve terraced storeys lies on the wider west end. Scharoun designed organic floor plans to open the latter building fan-like towards the sun, allowing residents of the 82 apartments to get into contact. In contrast to this, the nineteen-storey tall and compact Romeo block has a central L-shaped corridor, which provides access to 104 apartments and some studio apartments with big sloping windows on the highest floor. The lovers' exterior walls are made of exposed or multi-coloured concrete and clad with aluminium panels. Irregular triangular tapered balconies made of fibreglass and aluminium as well as projecting roofs give both buildings an expressive appearance.

049

LEO VETTER POOL
Leo Vetter Bad

REALISED 1956–1960
PLANNER Werner Gabriel
ADDRESS Landhausstrasse 192
ACCESS Open to the public

Located in the east of Stuttgart, the Leo Vetter Bad was the first swimming pool to be rebuilt after WW II. The pool replaced the original Stadtbad Ostheim, built in 1910. Named after Leo Vetter, founder of the 'Stuttgart Badgesellschaft', the building houses a multipurpose pool, a gym and bathroom facilities, and opens to a lawn in summer. The complex geometric design is topped by a kidney-shaped skylight and roof structure, supported by steel pillars reminiscent of light-weight reverse tripods. The raised skylight allows direct light onto the water surface and the integration of two diving boards. Besides the skylight, glass blocks and the glazed façade allow for light throughout the building. Facing Landhausstrasse, the building appears bar shaped and solid. The upper half of this façade is constructed of glass blocks and is decorated with metal sea animals. The entrance to the pool with its cubic overhang is also located here. The main pool hall was originally entirely surrounded by a brick and glass block façade. Upon renovation in 1998, glazed windows replaced the glass blocks in line with the geometric patterns.

NEARBY Workers Estate Ostenau (1914, Paul Bonatz, Karl Hengerer, Abelsbergstrasse, Landhausstrasse, Lehmgrubenstrasse), Church of the Sacred Heart (1934, Clemens Hummels, Schurwaldstrasse 1)

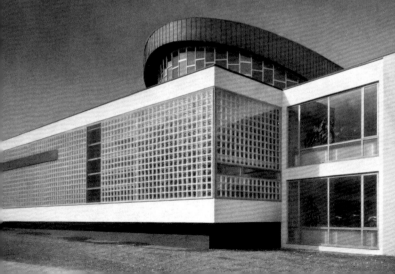

050

PROTESTANT RESURRECTION CHURCH
Evangelische Auferstehungskirche

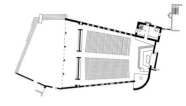

REALISED 1957

PLANNER Erwin Rohrberg

ADDRESS Haldenrainstrasse 200

ACCESS Open to the public

Built in 1957 by Erwin Rohrberg to serve 10,000 new citizens in the new district of Zuffenhausen-Rot this church is a prime example of the modern movement of the interwar period. The building with a trapezoidal floor plan consists of three volumes, giving it its shape and spatial perception: the long main volume of the church nave, added to a higher sanctuary and, standing out above it, the cubic bell tower. Entering the church resembles a light transition process, as first one arrives in a dimly lit forecourt leading to three bronzed gateways. From here the ceiling of the nave, elevated on round pillars, rises until the altar space, where the volumes of nave and sanctuary intersect and reach a height of almost 16 m. The two volumes are connected by an L-shaped window band, which reaches from the highest point down to the south where it meets the round sidewall of the chancel. Aligned and diagonally shifted roundels perforate the nave's as well as the tower's walls. At the top of the latter, small ocuil form rosettes reminiscent of gothic churches.

NEARBY Digital Local Switch of Deutsche Post AG (1990, Arno Lederer, Jórunn Ragnarsdóttir, Böckinger Strasse 31)

051

BADEN-WÜRTTEMBERG PARLIAMENT

Landtag von Baden-Württemberg

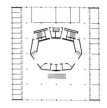

REALISED 1958–1961/2014–2016
PLANNER Kurt Viertel, Horst Linde, Erwin Heinle/Volker Staab, Werner Sobek
ADDRESS Konrad-Adenauer-Strasse 3
ACCESS Restricted

The Landtag—the first parliament constructed in Europe after WW II—was
built between 1958 and 1961 to contrast with its classical surroundings. Clear,
cubic, resolute: it reflects the architects' modern design language as well as
that of Ludwig Mies van der Rohe. Its transparency and openness made it a
symbol of the democratic system that defined the young republic of Germany.
Based on a roughly square plan, the 20 m-high and flat-roofed concrete frame
construction has a fully glazed ground floor that recedes behind concrete
columns. A modern metal glass curtain wall façade encloses both upper
floors. The vertical supports of the H-beam construction draw the outer skin
of the building and counter-balance the building's horizontality. On the upper
floors, all the vertical profiles are equally dimensioned. Only at the corners
the vertical profiles, which end the façades, do not join each other but leave
a continuous concrete column exposed. Materials were sourced to underline
the status of the programme, harmonise with the sandstone of the neighbouring buildings, and distinguish the project from average office complexes.

NEARBY State Theatre (Oberer Schlossgarten 6): Big House (1912, Max Littmann), Small House (1962, Hans Volkart), Extension Foyer (1984, Gottfried
Böhm)

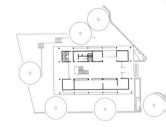

052

GERLING HOUSE
Gerling Haus

REALISED 1959–1960

PLANNER Rolf Gutbier with Hans Kammerer and Walter Belz

ADDRESS Herdweg 59

ACCESS Restricted

The Gerling House is an office building realised for an insurance group. It has a representative and solitaire character dissenting neither to the neighbouring buildings, nor to the urban situation, while it is reminiscent of the U.S. General Consulate. The long-stretched rectangular shaped, two-storey building is located in a very busy street zone between Lessing Strasse and Herdweg, narrowing in an acute angle. Placed parallel to Herdweg, its entrance is at the narrow side that opens towards Lessing Street. Round reinforced-concrete pillars painted in white elevate the first floor. Below, the ground floor recesses behind glass panes and black marble slabs giving the building a sense of lightness. The upper curtain-wall follows a strict pattern, dividing the surface into seventeen window axes along the long side and ten axes along the narrow side of the building. This rhythmic grid of the structure is further highlighted by silver aluminium double-T-profiles and white unpolished marble slabs that form the parapets. These materials give this building a very high-class, clean, strong and noble appearance, befitting the client's image.

NEARBY Eberhard-Ludwig Grammar School (1957, Hans und Adolf Bregler, Herdweg 72)

053

VOGELSANG SCHOOL
Vogelsangschule

REALISED 1959–1961

PLANNER Günter Behnisch, Bruno Lambart

ADDRESS Paulusstrasse 30

ACCESS None

It was the monumental size of the site that allowed the architects to design the Vogelsang school in small units. Eight single-storey pavilions and one three-storey main building surround a terraced playground. A further building with a sports hall and a school kitchen closes a gap on the eastern edge of the plot. The main idea was to bring each child—especially the youngest—to consider his class as a second home, being part of a school village and contributing to this village-life group. Each pavilion consists of a vestibule with a cloakroom, a classroom and a small multi-purpose room. The classrooms are glazed towards the south and additionally lit by skylight-bands to allow in as much sunlight as possible. Two pavilions are united under one wide fibre cement pitched-roof, creating four 'double-pavilions'. The dominating main building is a hall construction: three wings for classrooms and administration surround a double-height assembly hall. On its fourth side, a full square-panel glass façade framed between two brick walls provides visual contact with the outside. An inclined gable roof links the sections. The project has deep educational meaning as it was to be a democratic school, belonging to an international movement in pavilion schools led in Germany by Hans Scharoun and Behnisch's teacher Günter Willhelm.

NEARBY Paul-Gerhardt-Hof (1953, Paul Heim, Rosenbergstrasse 194)

054

BENSE HOUSE
Haus Bense

REALISED 1960
PLANNER Chen Kuen Lee
ADDRESS Eduard-Pfeiffer-Strasse 29
ACCESS None

The multiple dwelling, designed by Chen Kuen Lee in 1960, is located on a hill in the north of Stuttgart. Tucked into a steep slope and set back from the street, this special, organically shaped concrete building allows for a spacious garden, covering the garages inserted in the plot. The protruding balconies of the stacked, deconstructed volumes give the façade its briskness. The shape of the building plays with the surrounding elements, establishing a dialogue. This natural aspect of the exterior terraced concrete façade is the result of the interior composition. Chen Kuen Lee, former member of Hans Scharoun's office, designed the house with open and non-orthogonal free floor plans. Corresponding to specific functions, the interior space defines the outer shape of the dwelling, creating its asymmetrical, gradated levels. Hence, the house's architecture responds to the environment, the garden created by Hermann Mattern: the organic forms, a result of this balance, become extensions of the surrounding natural elements. Combining purpose, form, interior and exterior, Chen Kuen Lee sculpted a dialogue between architecture and nature.

NEARBY Rassbach Villa (1925, Paul Schmitthenner, Schottstrasse 98)

055

STOHRER OFFICE BUILDING
Bürohaus Stohrer

Third floor   First floor   Ground floor

REALISED 1961

PLANNER Paul Stohrer

ADDRESS Herdweg 64

ACCESS None

The architectural practice Paul Stohrer is situated at the intersection of Herdweg and Relenbergstrasse and provides three office floors and Stohrer's two-storey apartment on the top floor. The edifice borrows Le Corbusier's five points for new architecture, using pilotis, the free design of floor plans and façade, ribbon windows and a roof garden. On street level a pilotis structure lifts the building off the ground, creating free space and including a garage. Similarly, at the top a volume of sky is inserted between the roof and the walls. The appearance of the façade also stresses the lightness of the design. While the top floor remains hermetically closed, stepped behind a terrace with an opaque railing, the three levels below display ground-to-ceiling glass windows allowing for light inside. These horizontal lines of the curtain wall as well as ribbon windows create a horizontality, which is broken on the second floor. The gap there strengthens the horizontal tension and, synchronously punctuates the house's perfect, smooth cubic shape. Inside the open plan layout allows mobile walls and a melange of material surfaces.

NEARBY Eberhard-Ludwig Grammar School (1957, Hans und Adolf Bregler, Herdweg 72)

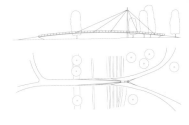

056

FERDINAND LEITNER PEDESTRIAN BRIDGE
Ferdinand-Leitner-Steg

REALISED 1961

PLANNER Fritz Leonhardt, Wolfhart Andrä

ADDRESS Schlossgarten crossing Gebhard-Müller-Platz

ACCESSIBILITY Open to the public

Consisting of an octagonal steel pylon and ten polyethylene cables attached to a concrete deck the Ferdinand Leitner Bridge, formerly known as Schiller Bridge, is a construction which spans a distance of almost 100 m. It connects the beginning upper castle gardens in the city centre with the much bigger middle and lower castle gardens passing the main station and finishing at the mineral baths near the river Neckar. The construction was realised for the national garden show (Bundesgartenschau) in 1961 and is an elegant example of Fritz Leonhardt's work with cable-stayed bridges, in this case in collaboration with Wolfhart Andrä. The arched configuration designed by the engineers increases in height at the centre, taking the path away from the traffic, enhancing the comfort for the pedestrians while crossing it. A noteworthy detail, that sets the build apart, is that on one of the sides the path bifurcates into two separate lanes softening the line of the bridge, spreading the flow of pedestrians in the park area and facilitating multiple access to it.

NEARBY State Theatre (Oberer Schlossgarten 6): Big House (1912, Max Littmann), Small House (1962, Hans Volkart), Extension Foyer (1984, Gottfried Böhm)

057

HAHN OFFICE TOWER
Hahn Hochhaus

REALISED 1962–1964
PLANNER Rolf Gutbrod
ADDRESS Friedrichstrasse 10
ACCESS Restricted

Even today this construction designed and constructed in the early 1960s by Rolf Gutbrod is still one of the most significant buildings in the area. As the design of the VW Porsche headquarters in Fellbach had won the architect critical acclaim, Hahn-Motorfahrzeuge GmbH commissioned him to design a centrally located head office fourteen storeys high. The building's most remarkable feature is its serrated, dynamic shape that contrasts with the symmetry of standard office buildings. The trapeziodial or polygonal office spaces are oriented to Friedrichstrasse and Keplerstrasse. The two main volumes are separated by a barrette structure which, from the outside, is only visible in the shape of the protruding cubic stairwell. Except for that, the façade's surface seems to be jagged, as ribbon windows and tilted concrete parapets alternate. Noteworthy too is the recessed and tilted glass cancel topping the entrance that has recently been redesigned as an event location by Atelier Brückner and can be rented for external events. Unfortunately, another feature, the multi-storey car showroom, has been lost.

NEARBY Kaufhof car park (2009, Transformation wulf architekten, Kronen-strasse 4)

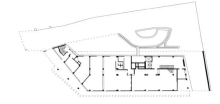

058

ZURICH-VITA HOUSE
Zürich-Vita-Haus

REALISED 1963–1965
PLANNER Wilfried Beck-Erlang
ADDRESS Paulinenstrasse 50
ACCESS Restricted

At an obtuse angle the elongated side of the six-storey building flanks Paulinenstrasse, while its narrow side just in front of the inner courtyard of the three-winged Rotebühlbau (regional tax office) faces Rotebühlstrasse. Most remarkable is the building's façade with its zick-zack-glass curtain. The frameless pre-stressed glass elements cover the rearward perpendicular load-bearing façade. The air permeable zone between the outer and inner glass front functions as climatic buffer and sound-absorber. It is the first example of a second-skin façade in Stuttgart. A restaurant and offices are located on the ground floor, further office facilities on the upper floors. The second-skin motif recurs in the shape of the artistically moulded glass-brick wall of the entrance. Like in other projects, the architect Beck-Erlang demonstrated his ability to respond sensitively to urban situations and to find unique answers for new emerging issues. Prior to the introduction of energy saving regulations, Beck-Erlang was already looking for innovative solutions for sustainable buildings.

NEARBY Tax office Rotebühlbau (1843, Johann Kasper Vogel, Ludwig Gaab, Rotebühlplatz 30)

059

BECK-ERLANG HOUSE
Haus Beck-Erlang

REALISED 1964–1966
PLANNER Wilfried Beck-Erlang
ADDRESS Planckstrasse 60
ACCESS None

In 1964 the architect Beck-Erlang purchased a small plot on Gänseheide for a reasonable price. The property has an awkward triangular layout and borders on the busy Planckstrasse as well as on the calmer Marquardt-strasse. However, exactly these urban restrictions inspired the architect for his exceptional design of a sculptural fair-faced concrete volume, housing office and living spaces on seven split levels. The rearward garden with a separate kitchen garden was filled up, covering an elongated garage. The entrance to the offices on the lower levels is at the southern building corner, leading to the single-storey reception area and the adjoining conference and ancillary rooms. Above it, volumes comprising half of the space of floors are staggered and protrude on the outside giving the feeling of interwoven elements. The stacked ateliers and Beck-Erlang's own office face Marquard-strasse. The latter is flanked by an outdoor single-flight staircase serving as entrance to the upper living area. Statically another rearward staircase links all split levels that merge like a fluent spatial continuum.

060

STATE ARCHIVE
Hauptstaatsarchiv

REALISED 1964–1969
PLANNER State Building Construction Office Baden-Württemberg
ADDRESS Konrad Adenauer Strasse 4
ACCESS Open to the public

Built between 1964 and 1969 the new state archive was meant to be the biggest in West Germany. It was intended to store and give access to documents from the 8th century until the present day. The two-storey rectangular construction containing several invisible lower levels encloses different facilities: record and research offices, reading areas and below ground level, hidden and well-guarded, a treasury for important archival materials. The archive is situated between two higher buildings, the State Library and the former Wilhelmspalais, today the City Museum. Free spaces and green areas exaggerate and harmonise the contrast between these volumes at the same time. Though the outline of the archive is quite simple—a cubic shape on a rectangular plan, two-storeys high with a flat roof clad with copper—the building is more complex than it seems. The subtle style of the ground floor made of clinker tiles allows one to appreciate the exposed concrete columns that bear the upper structure and make it 'float'. The inside of the archive itself resembles an atrium building. A reading area is located in the centre, surrounded by various functional rooms.

NEARBY Wilhelmspalais (1840 Giovanni Salucci, Conversion to City Library 1965, Wilhelm Tiedje, Conversion to City Museum 2018, LRO Lederer Ragnarsdóttir Oei, Konrad-Adenauer-Strasse 2)

061

STATE LIBRARY WÜRTTEMBERG
Württembergische Landesbibliothek

REALISED 1964–1970
PLANNER Horst Linde (State Building Construction
Office Baden-Württemberg)
ADDRESS Konrad Adenauer Strasse 6
ACCESS Open to the public

After its demolition in WW II the new edifice for the State Library Württemberg was erected based on the design of Horst Linde. Along with the State Archives the tripartite complex resurrects the pre-war cultural context at the former Neckarstrasse. In contrast to the previous neo-renaissance building, the new library consists of a simple cubic volume made of exposed concrete, topped by a copper roof. The raw external appearance is softened by clinker and cooper details; the window frames harmonise with the green exterior. On the inside, finely balanced, split-levels create a flowing spatial continuum of both high and wide as well as intimate spaces. Located on the ground floor are the cafeteria, an exhibition area and some workplaces. An extended ramp leads to the main foyer; from here stairs lead to the catalogue and the main reading area, surrounded by a gallery and tilted vertical ribbon windows. The 5.8 million historical and contemporary objects housed in this building are stored in two lower storeys. In 2011 the architects LRO Lederer Ragnarsdóttir Oei won the competition for the library's extension, which will be opened in 2018.

NEARBY Regional Court (1956, State Building Construction Office, Urban-strasse 18–20)

062

STUDIO HOUSE WÜRTTEMBERG ART ASSOCIATION
Atelierhaus Württembergischer Kunstverein

REALISED 1966–1969
PLANNER Paul Stohrer
ADDRESS Im Schellenkönig 56
ACCESS None

As early as the beginning of the 20ᵗʰ century the 'Verein Württembergischer Kunstfreunde' (Württemberg Association of Friends of Art) erected a building with studio spaces for artists on the slopes of Bopser. After its demolition in 1944, the prominent Stuttgart architect Paul Stohrer was commissioned to design a new studio house in its stead. He used the foundations of the old building for his cubic solution with nineteen studio apartments. Reminescent of Le Corbusier's Unité d'Habitation the single maisonette-apartments stretch from one side to the other, providing sufficient light for the tenants' art and allowing artists to focus on their work. Brick walls divide the façade into three distinct sections. Dark red bricks contrast with white concrete pilaster strips giving the façade a sense of rhythm. The façade on the valley side has box-shaped windows providing maximum northern light for the interior studio spaces. French balconies are enclosed by perforated sheet metal. The façade facing the hill covering the living spaces is more closed in character, yet, as the same box-shaped windows were used, coherence has been maintained.

NEARBY Reitzenstein Villa (1913, Hugo Schlösser, Johann Weirether, Richard-Wagner-Strasse 15)

063

IL INSTITUTE FOR LIGHTWEIGHT STRUCTURES

IL Institut für Leichtbau

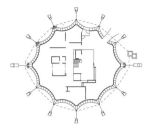

REALISED 1966–1969
PLANNER Frei Otto
ADDRESS Pfaffenwaldring 14
ACCESS Restricted

His tent construction for the German Exhibition Pavilion at the Expo in Montreal in 1967 (in collaboration with Rolf Gutbrod) not only gained Frei Otto international acclaim: it also revolutionised the construction of lightweight tensile structures worldwide. The one-to-one model he had built as a prototype on the campus of the University of Stuttgart became Frei Otto's permanent chair. The structure of this, the IL building (now ILEK), is comprised of steel tensile cables spanning the entire roof. These steel cables connect to a single steel shaft in the middle of the tent and to anchored points on the ground. The skin of the tent consists of boarded wood on the interior, grey fibre cement shingles on the exterior, and insulation. There is also a teardrop shaped sunroof made of glass acrylic panels, 'the eye', on the eastern portion of the roof, allowing natural light to flood the workshops inside. The interior has a terraced open plan with multiple levels towards the centre. A curved glass façade runs all along the circular building, which on the interior as well as exterior is dominated by three materials only: glass, steel and wood.

NEARBY Otto-Graf Institute Building (1962, Pfaffenwaldring 4), SimTECH Building, Informatics Research Centre, House of Students, (2016, Hartwig N. Schneider, Pfaffenwaldring 5)

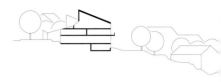

064

HOUSE OF BOYS CHOIR
Hymnus-Chorheim

REALISED 1967–1970
PLANNER Behnisch & Partner
ADDRESS Birkenwaldstrasse 98
ACCESS Restricted

The building is located on the steep slope below Birkenwaldstrasse, which enabled its multiple levels for different uses. The building has three main functions: kindergarten, post office, and rehearsal space for the choir. The form of the building is a comprised of three cubic volumes with pitched roofs that are broken and staggered in different ways. The volumes correspond with the three main functions of the building. The staggered lectern roofs arranged at different heights liven up the interior spaces. On the valley side of the building, the terraced balconies, different coloured ribbon windows with corrugated parapets, and aluminium skylights also help divide the façade into its three distinct volumes. Behnisch paid very close attention to detail when it came to the use and function of the building. The interior and exterior correlation of materiality and spatial layout distinguish the functionality needed for all aspects of the building respecting the child-orientated scale. The colours chosen for the interior and exterior create spatial boundaries without formal ties to the built structure.

065

GENO HOUSE
GENO Haus

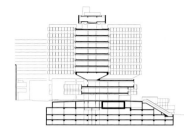

REALISED 1969–1972
PLANNER Kammerer + Belz
ADDRESS Heilbronner Strasse 41
ACCESS Restricted

The large up to eleven-storey glass cubes of GENO House (Cooperative Society) are a landmark at the entrance to Stuttgart in Heilbronner Strasse. The building complex was created after the fusion of two banks; its functions are therefore various: administration building, data centre, banking hall, canteen, cafeteria, kindergarten, self-service shop, not forgetting apartments and a 'Weinstube' (wine tavern). Hans Kammerer and Walter Belz interpreted the competition tasks as a small town in the city. They paid particular attention to pedestrians: a large ramp-like staircase leads from Heilbronner Strasse to the public space beneath the towers. To obtain enough space for this courtyard the office building cantilevers on the third floor. The façades consist of reflective solar control glass; the aim behind this was to reflect clouds and weather to foster a dematerialisation of the entire structure. Noteworthy is the supporting construction because of the intercepting reinforced concrete box girders on the upper floors.

NEARBY Arcotel Camino (1872, Georg Morlok, 2008, Christoph Mäckler, Heilbronner Strasse 31), Z-UP (2009, Wolfgang Kergaßner, Vordernbergstrasse 6), Milaneo (2014, RKW | Architektur + Städtebau, Mailänder Platz 7)

066

TAPACHSTRASSE RESIDENTIAL COMPLEX
Wohnsiedlung Tapachstrasse

REALISED 1969–1971
PLANNER Peter Faller, Hermann Schröder
ADDRESS Tapachstrasse 95
ACCESS None

Faller and Schröder experimented heavily with terraced buildings. Their design for the Tappachstrasse residence complex is an example of their 'Hillside Houses'. The main form of the project is comprised of two elongated and staggered concrete volumes overpowering in their Brutalist design, but very well thought out for an experimental mass housing complex. It consists of one building with six floors that are all terraced to the south, as well as smaller apartments scattered around the southern part of the site. The building has 80 terraced flats, and 19 atrium houses with nine different variations of three to five rooms each. To protect the courtyard and atriums from the upper storey views, the terrace homes were partially covered by wooden pergolas. The southern façade is comprised of the terraces split up by large concrete tilted slabs. The southern facing slabs are angled precisely to let in the perfect amount of sunlight to the apartments in the summer and winter, while the northern façade of the building is made of the walkways to the apartments and staircases as well as the entrance to the basement level parking.

067

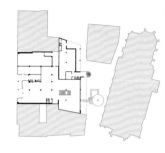

COMMERZBANK EXTENSION
Erweiterungsbau Commerzbank

REALISED 1970–1972
PLANNER Kammerer + Belz
ADDRESS Am Fruchtkasten 3
ACCESS Restricted

In 1970 the only plot available for the expansion of the Commerzbank AG branch on Königstrasse was a remaining construction gap used as a parking lot. It was needed for bank's new EDP system, canteen and as a garage. The planning objective was to expand the alley between Stiftstrasse and Schillerplatz and turn it into a small square with a fountain between the new structure, the Stiftskirche and Fruchtkasten. To achieve this, the extension building had to be set behind the building line. The redesign of the old Schillerplatz now based on an underground car park opened up the opportunity to connect the small and the large space to form a reasonable ensemble where old and new correlate. The almost black and smooth house reflects the old structures around it in its large windows and glass tower. The latter houses the building's staircase and divides the façade in two-fifths to the left and in three fifths to the right. While the right part is plain, the left side of the façade reveals more plasticity as it staggers backwards from the ground floor to the third floor to broaden the public space.

068

STUDENT HOUSING PFAFFENHOF I + PFAFFENHOF II
Studentenwohnheim Pfaffenhof I + Pfaffenhof II

REALISED 1966–1972
PLANNER Atelier 5
ADDRESS Pfaffenwaldring 42–48
ACCESS Open to the public

In 1965 the well-known Swiss architectural studio Atelier 5 won a tender with a modern concept for a big student housing project. The project consisted of four blocks of buildings with 610 rooms. The buildings are arranged asymmetrically and intermittently, so that the resulting green spaces between them create a peaceful and natural atmosphere. The architects sought an impression of variety in each of the buildings' design, but also to make them part of a single whole. Each building has different heights, volumes and a different arrangement of rooms reflected in the changing height of the windows and painted wood and fibre cement panels covering the external exposed concrete structure. The resulting apparent disorganisation gives them a chaotic appearance but the right-angled, cubistic style of each building follows an inner sense of order. The buildings' interiors are arranged in compartments. Bathrooms and kitchens are clustered to avoid noise and to support social exchange. Student's rooms are divided into thematic areas: on the outer wall there is a desk and wardrobe, on the opposite side a bed and wash-basin.

NEARBY Laboratories for Materials Testing (MPA) (1969, Friedrich Wagner, Pfaffenwaldring 32), Natural Sciences Centre (NWZ) (1974, Universitätsbauamt, Pfaffenwaldring 45–47)

Just as the Concert Hall was an internationally acclaimed incunabulum of the 1950s, the New State Gallery marks the beginning of postmodern architecture in Germany. As early as 1972, the extension of the Commerzbank at the Fruchtkasten had addressed the topic of building in a historical context. The 1975 European Heritage Year and the realisation that a city is for people, not for cars, led to a change in urban planning. The redevelopment of Calwer Steet Quarter and its Passage proved that old and new can merge. A further step in this direction was the redevelopment of the 'Bohnenviertel' (1979–87), in which the original combination of functions and particularly living in the city were successfully preserved. The conversion of Königstrasse into a pedestrian zone (Behnisch & Partner, 1982) revised the prioritisation of car traffic and went hand in hand with the first competitions for the reorganisation of the Kleiner Schlossplatz, which, ten years after its opening, had already lost its significance as a building for transportation. The expansion of the tram into a subway system (Schlossplatz station by Behnisch & Partner, 1978) and the construction of the S-Bahn relieved the streets of traffic. The area between Neckarstrasse and Kernerplatz was restructured by a large concave building complex housing the Hotel Meridien and some

ministries (Kammerer + Belz, Kucher und Partner, 1988). Other than that, there were no coherent urban development measures in the inner city. Ideas to reorganise pre-war density and to dismantle the major transport axes remained theoretical (Rob Krier, 1975). On the other hand, architects such as Gottfried Böhm were given the opportunity to create small and large buildings (State Theatre with dome, 1984, administrative building for Züblin AG, 1984). The sculptor Otto Herbert Hajek, whose strongly coloured, large-format steel sculptures can be found on many squares, designed the Leuze Spa (1983) in a particularly expressive form. Peter Hübner experimented with participatory construction at the youth hostels in Wangen (1984) and Stammheim (1990). With the Luginsland kindergarten (1990) Günter Behnisch & Partner planned the first deconstructivist construction in Germany.

After the great achievements and efforts of the reconstruction and the boom years, the years after the Heritage Year 1975, in which demography and economy had reached a certain growth limit, led to a decentralised urban planning and an upgrading of the suburban centres. In the inner city itself, Königstrasse exemplified how pedestrianised zones can raise the quality of life in the city.

069

BROADCASTING CENTRE STUTTGART
Stuttgarter Funkhaus

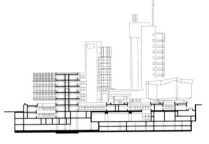

REALISED 1972–1977
PLANNER Rolf Gutbrod
ADDRESS Neckarstrasse 230
ACCESS Restricted

Rolf Gutbrod's design for the Stuttgart broadcasting house had to satisfy a number of needs and demands. It was to be a radio broadcasting studio, had to adapt to the rapid development of TV broadcasting, had to fit the urban surrounding of the Villa Berg park area, and had to embody the broadcasting studio as a public good. To achieve this, the building was broken up into three volumes (for communication, editorial staff, administration and production), which move towards and against each other. This makes the building appear differently when viewed from different angles. The construction plays with contrasting elements: a rather cold façade contrasts with playful details such as the mosaic on the garden terrace or the triangulated window, which lets light into the lowest level of the broadcasting studios. This 'Auge Gottes' (God's Eye) is the most important element of the complex besides the colouring and varying materials indicating different areas. The floor plan displays no symmetrical or right-angled elements. The segmented complex with its blue and silver façade is still one of the most important broadcasting studios.

NEARBY Villa Berg (1845, Christian von Leins, Villa Berg 1)

070

GUEST LECTURERS' HOUSE
Gastdozentenwohnhaus

REALISED 1973–1976
PLANNER Lutz & Wick
ADDRESS Relenbergstrasse 57
ACCESS Restricted

The concrete residential tower for visiting lecturers from abroad is located on the upper edge of university campus looking over the city. It was built by the architects Hans-Dieter Lutz and Roland Wick, who had worked for Rolf Gutbier (the former rector of the Technical University of Stuttgart) until they founded their own office. The tower is a prime example of 1970s brutalism, has 16 storeys, a total height of almost 50 m and a roof terrace. The bearing structure consists of reinforced concrete, allowing for a free façade design in exposed concrete. The façade is broken up into big vertical volumes and subdivided. The massive concrete parapets of the balconies add to the monumental effect. An exterior access tower houses the lifts, which service every third level only and whose doors open onto a balcony. The occupants of the levels below and above the lift-exit reach the one- to four-room apartments via two internal staircases. The stairs themselves are made of solid concrete elements and were later given an artificial stone covering that contrasts with the brutalism as do the aluminium composite windows.

NEARBY Villengärten (2016, Kuehn Malvezzi, Relenbergstrasse 51, Seestrasse 71–75, Wiederholdstrasse 15a–c), House at Seestrasse (2008, Wilford Schupp Architekten, Seestrasse 92, Relenbergstrasse 37–39)

071

CAMPUS CANTEEN STUTTGART-VAIHINGEN

Mensa der Universität Stuttgart-Vaihingen

REALISED 1973–1976
PLANNER Atelier 5
ADDRESS Pfaffenwaldring 45
ACCESS Open to the public

The architects' vision was to create a canteen that would be a space to hang out and not merely a place to eat, a place for student communication and get-together. Separating the hall into small-scale units by using a tight construction grid, it has an almost private character. The entire five-storey building bases on a 3.20 m × 3.20 m grid, from the concrete framework up to the dimensions of a dining table for 5 people on each side, which results in 1,200 seating spots, one restaurant, a cafeteria for 500 people and a lounge area. Roland Gfeller-Corthes created the interior design; his chairs, lighting and colouring contribute to the intended clubhouse character. The ground floor hosts storage and technical facilities, a bowling alley, bookstore, shop and lounge area facing the 'Lernstrasse' (learning street). This floor is supposed to be the most frequented place, while the intermediate floors are for calmer activities. Atriums connect all floors visually and deny the building's strict separation into single areas. The façade and the roof mirror the inside functions, the height varies accordingly.

NEARBY Laboratories for Materials Testing (MPA) (1969, Friedrich Wagner, Pfaffenwaldring 32), Natural Sciences Centre (NWZ) (1974, Universitätsbauamt, Pfaffenwaldring 45–47)

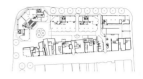

072

CALWER STREET QUARTER AND CALWER PASSAGE

Stadtquartier Calwer Strasse und Calwer Passage

REALISED 1974–1978
PLANNER Kammerer + Belz und Partner
ADDRESS Calwer Strasse and Calwer Passage
ACCESS Open to the public

The question-marks raised in the redevelopment of post-war Stuttgart led to the detailed design of this quarter, in which the old houses on Calwer-Strasse were connected with the new construction on Theodor-Heuss-Strasse. A major building forms the centre of the infrastructure hub on Rotebühlstrasse and marks the end of Theodor-Heuss-Strasse. A small square emerges at the back, leading to the U-and S-Bahn and serving as the main entrance for the new passage. This passage, which connects the old houses with the new construction, was the first post-war passage in Europe, continuing the passage architecture of the 19th century and triggering a passage hype all over Europe for the next ten years. The glass roof seamlessly connects the 'new' with the 'old'. The gables on the old side are confronted with maisonette apartments on the new side. There is a unique mixture of living and working areas in this quarter, achieving the ideal of a lively city. A lot of effort was put into the conservation of the old houses, but due to the new building regulations, nothing more than atmospheric covers could be preserved.

NEARBY Tax office Rotebühlbau (1843, Johann Kasper Vogel, Ludwig Gaab, Rotebühlplatz 30)

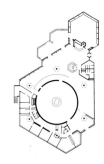

073

CARL ZEISS PLANETARIUM
Carl-Zeiss-Planetarium

REALISED 1975–1977
PLANNER Wilfried Beck-Erlang
ADDRESS Neckarstrasse 47
ACCESS Open to the public

The first Stuttgart planetarium was opened in May 1928. It was equipped with a ZEISS Model II projector and housed in a dome on the former Hindenburgbau opposite the main station. After its destruction in 1943, the Carl Zeiss Foundation laid the foundation for today's planetarium and donated a Zeiss VI-A projector to the city of Stuttgart. The new building, which displays the remains of its predecessor, reopened in April 1977. Technical aesthetics dominate the design: the structure has the shape of a hexagonal truncated stepped pyramid, whose dome is suspended from precast concrete elements on a steel grid. The abutment of a spider-like metal construction serves six detached concrete pillars in the foyer. Despite its sound-insulating and reflective façade that lets it blend in with its surroundings, the planetarium achieves a distinctive presence. Inspired by the Parisian Centre Pompidou (1977) the construction visualises the postmodern and technophilic atmosphere and aerospace euphoria after the moon landing of Apollo 11. In this respect, the planetarium marks a turning point in the oeuvre of its architect Beck-Erlang.

NEARBY Interior Ministry (2013, Volker Staab Architekten, Willy-Brandt-Strasse 41)

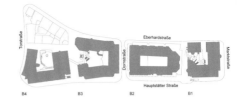

074

SWABIAN CENTRE
Schwabenzentrum

REALISED 1978–1985
PLANNER Kilpper + Partner, Rödl + Kieferle
ADDRESS Eberhardstrasse, Hauptstätterstrasse,
Torstrasse, Dornstrasse, Marktstrasse
ACCESS Restricted

With the completion of the Schwabenzentrum the last major war-related va-
cant lot of inner Stuttgart was filled. Of Hans Scharoun's 1970s original design
of a 16-storey terrace-housing complex called 'Schwabenzentrum' only the
name was kept—though it was featured in several articles and magazines.
The winning design of the local competition was a four to six- storey building
complex with courtyards, which could be adapted in height and shape to the
surrounding buildings. Kilpper and Partners designed the stone-clad B1, B2
and B4 with their metal detailing; Rödl + Kieferle created B3. B2, built in 1983,
contains a courtyard with stairs and terraced walkways down to the Rathaus
tram stop. It is the largest building of the Schwabenzentrum complex. Its
upper floors house offices (belonging to city administration), and below are
shops and restaurants as well as an underground car park. B3 was built from
1982–1984 and was created for the offices of the municipal administration
with apartments on the top floor. Over 50 shops and restaurants have con-
tributed to the revitalisation of the complex.

NEARBY Hegel-House Memorial (16th century/1991, Stuttgart Building Construction Office, Eberhardstrasse 53)

075

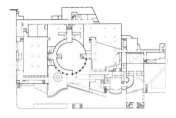

NEW STATE GALLERY
Neue Staatsgalerie

REALISED 1979–1984
PLANNER James Stirling, Michael Wilford and Associates
ADDRESS Konrad-Adenauer-Strasse 30–32
ACCESS Open to the public

With his design for the New State Gallery James Stirling not only won the architectural competition in 1977, but also evoked a fundamental debate on postmodernism vs modern architecture. His design connected the Old State Gallery (1843) with the new one and fits into the landscape. Two L-shaped volumes are ordered in a symmetrical U-shape around an open rotunda. This spiralling promenade around an outdoor sculpture area connects the large terrace facing the city to the residential areas behind it. The terrace becomes an elevated pedestrian walk linking the museums to the other major institutions along the busy road. Beneath the terrace level is the car park, which has ventilation openings that look like misplaced bricks. Placed in front of the building, a tall steel pavilion accentuates the ascent to the entrance level. Floor plan and façades use traditional elements, but interpret them in a new way. Travertine and sandstone are combined with sometimes brightly coloured industrial steel to emphasise the timeless, yet, evolving art and architecture. The curved glass entrance façade, held by a green steel frame, reflects the surroundings.

NEARBY State Theatre (Oberer Schlossgarten 6): Big House (1912, Max Littmann), Small House (1962, Hans Volkart), Extension Foyer (1984, Gottfried Böhm)

076

TOWN HOUSES
Stadthäuser

REALISED 1980–1982
PLANNER John Darbourne & Geoffrey Darke, Ulfert Weber
ADDRESS Charlottenstrasse, Rosenstrasse
ACCESS Restricted

Home to winemakers and the trades in previous centuries, the Bohnenviertel (Bean Quarter) is one of the oldest parts of Stuttgart. After WW II, initial plans to erect a technical town hall in the destroyed area failed. To this day the district has kept its characteristic small-scale urban layout and mixed use, thanks to a reference framework created in the mid-1970s for an enclosed perimeter block development that integrated the existing buildings. It stipulated that the ground floors should be for commercial use, upper floors for residential use. Green courtyards, private gardens and traffic-calmed streets, playgrounds and meeting places were to give the area a community atmosphere. The British office Darbourne & Darke and the Stuttgart architect Ulfert Weber won the competition for the first stage in 1977. Their design pursued the idea of the stackable dwelling reminiscent of the English town house to adapt to the historical environment in scale and material. It provides stores and offices on the ground floors as well as 51 flats of 2-5 ½ rooms with individual access from the courtyards. A parking lot extends underneath the development.

NEARBY Leonhardt's Church (1468/1954, Aberlin Jörg/Rudolf Lempp, Konrad Schneeweiß, Leonhardsplatz 26), Gustav Siegle House (1912, Theodor Fischer/1954, Martin Elsaesser, Leonhardsplatz 28)

077

HANNS-MARTIN SCHLEYER
SPORTS DOME
Hanns-Martin-Schleyer-Halle

REALISED 1980–1983

PLANNER Siegel, Wonneberg + Partner

ADDRESS Mercedesstrasse 69

ACCESS Restricted

This multi-functional sport dome was constructed as the greatest in Europe at that time. The basic shape is defined by the racing cycle track. It forms two straight parallel tracks on the long sides with semi-circular curves on the shorter sides. As the level of the ground floor is aligned to the height of the sloped semi-circular curves, this level has been raised by 5 m. This is why the main entrances for the public can only be reached via a platform with connecting ramps and stairs. From the main entrance visitor flow is directed to the tribune at the long sides of the track. The permanent stalls accommodate 4,884 visitors inside the dome and 2,959 additional people can be fitted in when the cycle racing track is dismantled. With its 200 m track, the sport dome can also house athletics events. The dome is a pre-stressed concrete construction containing steel trusses, spanning 65 m across its centre. A shed-roof brings natural light into the arena; however, in order to avoid direct light the shed-roof is aligned to the north and rotated by 30 degrees off the orientation of the dome.

NEARBY Mercedes-Benz Arena (1933/1938/1973/2006, Bonatz & Scholer/ Stuttgart Building Construction Office / Siegel, Wonneberg + Partner, Arat, Siegel + Partner, Mercedesstrasse 87)

078

HERBERT-KELLER HOUSE
Herbert-Keller-Haus

REALISED 1981–1984
PLANNER Behnisch & Partner
ADDRESS Heilbronner Strasse 180
ACCESS Restricted

Two contradictory challenges led to the shape of this building: on the one hand, the effort of the developer to gain maximum square footage and to maximise profit. On the other hand, the client was the 'Diakonisches Werk', a non-profit organisation working with socially vulnerable people. This inner conflict is reflected in the architecture of this building. The structural framework—derived from the underground parking—is rational, highly technological and stringent. The parts of the building, however, which act and interact with the clients, are open, imperfect, weak and perceptive. This results in a large overall system displaying a multitude of individual solutions. Meeting rooms do not adhere to the straight grid but form organic shapes. The cafeteria on the ground floor floats into a small indoor garden, blurring the borders. Corridors are not straight, but open up and then narrow again to form niches and open space. The inner order of the building structure and its facilities is not hierarchical. There should be no artificial language, but honesty in materiality and design. Load bearing steel trusses are strong and heavy. Wood is wood and not veneer.

079

STATE MUSEUM OF NATURAL HISTORY AT LÖWENTOR
Staatliches Museum für Naturkunde am Löwentor

REALISED 1981–1985
PLANNER Siegel, Wonneberg + Partner
ADDRESS Rosensteinstrasse 1, Nordbahnhofstrasse 190
ACCESS Open to the public

Half-submerged at the edge Rosensteinpark sits a squat complex—the current Natural History museum. As the museum's site at Neckarstrasse had been destroyed in WW II, the state of Baden-Württemberg announced a competition in 1973. The newly built museum complex was completed twelve years later. Two different structural designs were created that were integrated above and below ground with an intervening entrance courtyard, which characterises the appearance of the complex on Nordbahnhofstrasse. The volume holding the collection on display in the northern side is designed as a monolithic concrete block; the side facing the road is closed, whereas courtyard and park face toward the inside. On the southern side are the work and research areas with their horizontal layout and delicate metal-glass-wood architecture that create a strong contrast and a good transition to the park. The entrance courtyard is a reception room. Its paved marble 'time track' and the distorted steel dinosaurs by Bernhard Luginbühl, invite visitors to visit the museum and lead to the deeper green space.

NEARBY Rosenstein Castle Museum (1829, Giovanni Salucci, Rosensteinpark)

080

HYSOLAR RESEARCH INSTITUTE BUILDING

HYSOLAR Forschungsinstitut

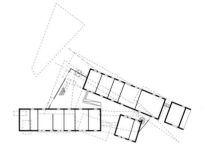

REALISED 1986–1987
PLANNER Behnisch & Partner
ADDRESS Allmandring 19
ACCESS None

The HYSOLAR building was designed for research into turning solar energy into energy-storing hydrogen. The importance and innovation of this sophisticated technology influenced the architecture of this building that originally housed the Institute of Physical Electronics and the Institute of Thermodynamics as well as the German Aerospace Research and Testing Establishment (DFLR). Furthermore, the project was small enough for formal experiments using an array of different unmodified, mostly prefabricated industrial products in a free spatial balance. This 'spatial collage of ready-mades' (Günter Behnisch) formed a new accent on the university campus and was to become one of the most radical deconstructivistic buildings in Germany. Two storeys of stacked and rowed containers meet at an acute angle. The V-shaped inter-space forms an open hall. Lateral boundaries of glass cause the expansive steel roof to float. Protruding coloured elements of façade and the load-bearing construction as well as the plastic cladding intensify the building's dynamic, vivacious and furious character.

NEARBY Centre for Virtual Engineering (ZVE), Fraunhofer Society, 2012, UN Studio and ASPLAN, Nobelstrasse 12

1990–Today

Looking at Stuttgart's urban development since 1990, one could put forward the hypothesis that the city was actually finished and required only a few minor interventions to enhance the quality of the quarters and neighbourhoods. The International Garden Exhibition IGA 1993 created a green corridor from the Rosensteinpark up to the Killesberg and construction projects such as the EXPO 'Habitation 2000' at Nordbahnhof and the studios in Reitzensteinstrasse (Fritz and Elisabeth Barth, 1993). Close by, the Wilhelma farm (cheret bozic, 1993) was the first to experiment with LVL (Laminated Veneer Lumber) as a supporting construction material. Werner Sobek created his private residence R 128 (2000) as a modular, glazed building which is 100% sustainable. Protected historic buildings and other conversion projects shaped the cityscape. The Kronen-Carré (Auer Weber, 2001) close to the main station kicked off the development of further conversion projects in the city centre with the Dorotheen-Quartier (Behnisch Architekten, 2017) next to the market hall being the youngest of these projects. Two major shopping centres, the Milaneo (RKW | Architecture + Urban Development, 2014) behind the main station and the Gerber (EPA Planungsgruppe GmbH/Bernd Albers, 2014) in the west of the old town, compete with the shops of the inner city.

In order to reduce the increased traffic load, the city is focusing on internal development and reutilisation projects in underused areas like the Baur area and the ParkQuartier in Stuttgart Berg (2007), the Killesberg Höhe (Baumschlager Eberle, Chipperfield, KCAP and Ortner & Ortner, 2013), the Villengärten at the Relenberg (Kuehn Malvezzi, 2017) or the Rosenberg-höfe (willwersch architekten, 2017) in Breitscheidstrasse, to mention just a few. By upgrading the streets and squares, the city is steadily gaining urban quality, though the transport concept lags behind. Still exemplary are the New State Gallery, the State College of Music and the history museum (Stirling Wilford, Schupp, Gerstner). Together with the converted Wilhelms-palais and the new extension of the State Library by LRO Lederer Ragnars-dottir Oei (2017/18) the buildings of the 'Kulturmeile' (cultural mile) take up Stirling's ideas of cross-linking the cultural institutions with the castle gardens. At times, however, there are also small projects and interventions, which contribute to improving the quality of the street space, such as the transformation of the Kaufhof car park in Kronenstrasse by wulf architek-ten in 2009. The really important themes of our time—mobility, carbon neutrality, sustainability—will be addressed by the International Building Exhibition planned for the year 2027.

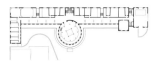

081

STATE COLLEGE OF MUSIC AND PERFORMING ARTS

Staatliche Hochschule für Musik und Darstellende Kunst

REALISED 1987–1996

PLANNER James Stirling, Michael Wilford and Associates

ADDRESS Urbanstrasse 25

ACCESS Restricted

In the post-war era a master plan for a 'Kulturmeile' (cultural mile) was drawn up, which today comprises the Old and New State Gallery, the Chamber Theatre and the State College of Music and Performing Arts juxtaposed along a pedestrian path on Konrad-Adenauer-Strasse. The State College was erected in the second construction stage of this project, based on Stirling's and Wilford's draft. Its design reflects a greater composition: its floor plan mirrors the L-shape of the Chamber Theatre. Its central and most dominant element, the squat, 'stumpy' tower reflects Stuttgart's numerous towers and the open rotunda of the State Gallery. The tower contains a three-storey high concert hall, a library and a senate hall. A curved ramp wraps around the base and leads to the main entrance. There is a publicly accessible roof terrace at the top. The materials used for the façade are similar to those of the State Gallery, but implemented in a different way: while the gallery's appearance is predominantly compact and introverted, the varying patterns of window openings generate greater transparency for the State College. Inside numerous wooden elements cater to acoustic needs.

082

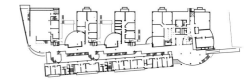

ROTEBÜHLPLATZ
MEETING POINT
Treffpunkt Rotebühlplatz

REALISED 1988–1992
PLANNER Horst Haag
ADDRESS Rotebühlplatz 28
ACCESS Open to the public

The competition for the Rotebühlplatz Meeting Point was won by the office of Horst Haag in 1979. The elongated five-storey building on top of an underground car park houses several cultural facilities on approx. 9,000 m² and is frequented by up to 3,000 visitors daily. An 80 m long and 24 m wide hall forms its centre and 'backbone'. Covered with a glass-roof, the hall, stretching all along the building, serves as pedestrian area, which has connecting stairwells, balconies and seating areas. Ateliers, rehearsal rooms of the Stuttgart Music School and a media library are located in the front part of the building at Rotebühlplatz. Behind this hemispheric part, the building is divided into four transverse wings intersected by three greened patios. This part of the building houses the classrooms of the Volkshochschule (adult education centre) and a cafeteria. A mix of precast concrete blocks (also used inside), glass and metal characterises the façade. The flat roofs have been greened. The technical installations of the building are partially displayed on the façade. Galvanised steel tubes enhance the building's workshop-like character.

083

WILHELMA ZOO ANNEXES
Wilhelma Zoo Erweiterungsbauten

REALISED 1988–2013
PLANNER Auer Weber Architekten; cheret
bozic architekten; Hascher Jehle Architektur
ADDRESS Wilhelma 13
ACCESS Open to the public

At the command of King Wilhelm I and designed as a private zoo by the architect Karl Ludwig Zanth several Moorish style buildings—which still form the core of the Wilhelma today—were erected from 1846–1866. Plans for an even more generous complex were changed several times for financial reasons and heavy public protest. After WW I the zoo was opened to the public; in the 1960s it was combined with the botanical garden. Demolitions during WW II and the demand for new attractions called for new structures and additions like for instance the Great Aviary (1993), the Show Farm (1993), the Amazonia House (2000), the Wilhelma School (2011) as well as the new Ape House (2013).

Beginning with the Great Aviary, the architects' office Auer Weber translated the brief for a collective house for twelve bird species into a delicate lightweight structure of a tensed cable net between high and low points giving it an uneven and highly transparent appearance. The Amazonia House, the office's second project in Wilhelma Zoo, allows an insight into rainforest flora and fauna. Greenhouse-like, a half-barrel vault leans onto a sloped pane creating a volume of 66 m by 18 m and 14 m in height. The tensioned arch supports the modular glass grid including ventilation elements as well as a light external frame for sun protection stores.

For the IGA 1993 the Stuttgart architects cheret bozic designed the show farm with the first load-bearing roof construction of veneer laminated wood. Later they were commissioned to create the new Wilhelma School: a square pavilion-like construction made of prefabricated concrete elements holding a thin roof. It was to be embedded inconspicuously into the existing context and to offer various insights at the same time and therefore features surrounding ceiling-high windows. The inner core contains sanitary facilities that divide the building into a big seminar space and a back office.

The latest construction, the Ape House by Hascher Jehle Architektur, offers vast interior spaces and big exterior areas specifically designed for the different ape species as well as generous visitor areas. Outside the concrete building has a hill-like appearance and is partially covered in grass. The exterior areas for the animals are canopied with a steel net, fixed to high galvanised steel poles. Inside, a linear visitors' path allows a glimpse into the apes' spaces on one side and to the outside through ceiling-high glazing on the other. The interior is finished in raw concrete and tree-like slender concrete pillars support the roof. Plants frame the glass separation between monkeys and visitors, providing associations to the natural habitat of the apes.

084

EXPO 'HABITATION 2000'
Expo 'Wohnen 2000'

REALISED 1991–1993

PLANNER Terrace houses at Sarweystrasse: ECD Partnership (40–44); Elzbieta Muszynska, Krysztof Muszynska, Lech Baranski/Bildingmeier, Egenhofer, Dübbers (46–52); Johs Gunnarshaug (60–64); Karla Szyszkowitz-Kowalski, Michael Szyszkowitz (54–58); HHS Architekten (72–76); Jourda et Perraudin Partenaires (66–70) / Multi-family dwellings at Störzbachstrasse: Gullichsen Kairanno Vormala Arkkitehditky (11); Tegnestuen Vandkunsten (13); Dieter Schempp (15); Bengt Warne, Jo Glässel (17); Entwurfsgruppe Stahr (19); Michael Alder (21); Mecanoo (23–27)

ADDRESS Sarweystrasse 40–76, Störzbachstrasse 11–27

ACCESS Restricted

In 1993 the International Gardening Exhibition (IGA) entitled 'Responsibility towards the Nature in the City' prompted the architecture exposition 'Habitation 2000' displaying projects by thirteen architects and architect teams, who had all been finalists of an international competition in 1988. The site allocated to the project is next to the Nordbahnhof and has several infrastructural constraints. Hence, the aim was to explore the simultaneous embedding of new constructions into the existing context and the creation of innovative living forms in combination with current ecological technologies for a sustainable and energy sufficient architecture. These aims were transferred into conservatories used as climatic or soundproofing buffer, timber as building material, the green, flat roofs and the experimental use of solar technology, which—at that time—was in its infancy. The proposed site was separated into two areas: seventeen terrace houses at Sarweystrasse and seven multi-storey family dwellings along Störzbachstrasse.

The character of the two areas differs: the park-like composition of six groups of terrace houses with three to four units each has a homely feel to it—six inventive solutions of the common terrace house. In some of the designs the single units appear as single houses, in others they fuse to one united volume with a continuous configuration of roof and façades. Note-worthy is the design by the Norwegian architect Gunnarshaug, whose three east-west orientated, expanded saddle roof houses with glass-covered courtyards in their middle reflect on urban density. The design of HHS architects focuses on the ecological aspect; here a high and expanded glass pane leans against three simple cubes to create a conservatory. Rotatable solar panels are used for heating as well as natural shading when needed. The most expressive design is the deconstructive approach of the Austrian architects' couple Szyszkowitz-Kowalski and Szyszkowitz with its sophisticated arrangement of intersecting, protruding and returning elements.

Innovative organisation of the apartment layouts and the stimulation of social exchange characterise the designs of the aligned, multi-family houses. The dwelling of the Finnish architects at Störzbachstrasse 11 offers two-storey loggia-like conservatories in front of maisonettes, the Danish architects Warne and Glässel pursue the theme of a collective atrium ascending the variable flats. Designed by the Dutch office Mecanoo, three slender residence towers, that are accessed and connected by balconies and a free-standing lift, enjoyed much critical acclaim.

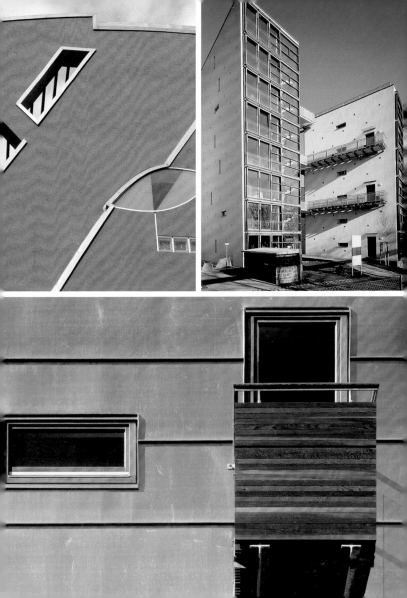

085

BOMBAY AND BRÜNNER PEDESTRIAN BRIDGES

Bombaystege und Brünner Steg

REALISED 1992

PLANNER Planungsgruppe Luz, Lohrer, Egenhofer, Schlaich

ADDRESS Heilbronnerstrasse, Nordbahnhof

ACCESS Open to the public

The two pedestrian bridges built for the International Gardening Exhibition (IGA) in 1993 connect the Killesberg and Leibfriedscher Park, bridging railway tracks and the busy Heilbronner Strasse. Y-shapes dominate the layout when viewed from above. Suspended from a steel mast in the centre, Bombaystege leads to a central metro station. The symmetrical Brünner Steg connects both sides of the tracks with the train station in the middle. Although the bridges are independent structures they only make sense together as one allows the crossing of the tracks while the other provides the connection across the nearby street in the northwest. Also structurally both bridges are similar. One single big steel mast from which six cables hold the decks transfers all loads to the ground. The spans of the two bridges are approximately 30 m and 120 m. While the mast of the Brünner Steg is balanced by the symmetrical loads of the bridge itself, the mast of the Bombaystege needs additional fixing as it is at the centre of the Y-section. Its wide ranging south-eastern wing links the park scenery to Nordbahnhof station.

SERVICE CENTRE OF LANDESGIROKASSE STUTTGART AT BOLLWERK

Haus der Dienstleistungen der Landesgirokasse Stuttgart am Bollwerk

REALISED 1992–1997
PLANNER Behnisch, Sabatke, Behnisch
ADDRESS Fritz-Elsass-Strasse 31
ACCESS Restricted

The bank received a plot near the 'Bollwerk' bastion in exchange for a planned high-rise near the Old Riding Hall in the 1980s. In 1991 Behnisch, Sabatke, Behnisch won the competition with a common perimeter block development as its basic design. But in the vertical axis the construction exhibits its diversification. The buildings' height varies between five and nine storeys with the middle part being cut out to provide natural lighting. The ground floor facing the street houses a bank, a restaurant and a cinema. Towards Fritz-Elsass-Strasse the building is visually broken up. The four irregular wings surround a patio with a small pond. A two-storey cone-shaped glass façade, roofing the cafeteria, is continued through the patio. By grading and rotating of the office floors the design fights uniformity. Particularly prominent is the protruding space to hold executive receptions at the top of the building. The entrance hall underneath is covered by a large inclined glass façade. The uniform grid of the façade, interacting with the playfully arranged coloured breastworks, gives the building a sophisticated appearance.

NEARBY Congress Hall (1991, Wolfgang Henning, Berliner Platz 3)

087

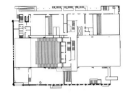

THEATRE HOUSE STUTTGART
Theaterhaus Stuttgart e.V.

REALISED 1999–2003
PLANNER plus + bauplanung GmbH Hübner – Forster
Hübner und egelhard.eggler.architekten
ADDRESS Siemensstrasse 11
ACCESS Open to the public

Along the northern arterial road to Stuttgart, an industrial area had been established in the course of the 20th century which got run down in the 1990s. An international competition for urban development won by Steidle & Partner Munich presented ideas for a conversion into a mixed service area. For one of the main structures, an industrial hall built by Emil Fahrenkamp in 1923, there was the suggestion to use it as a cultural venue with various play and production facilities of different sizes. From this listed building parts of the outer walls and the roofing construction are still preserved. The new additions are carefully integrated so as to form a new unity. A multifunctional hall, a theatre and concert hall providing 1000 seats, three additional theatres and four rehearsal rooms are complemented by various workshops. The lengthy foyer connects to all the rooms. Simple materials and visible construction also convey the industrial character of the building. The Theatre House has become a cultural hotspot of Stuttgart. The architects succeeded in combining old and new structures, which allows the two layers of time to express themselves on the same level.

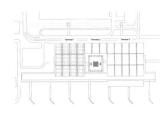

088

STUTTGART AIRPORT TERMINALS 1–3
Flughafen Stuttgart Terminal 1–3

REALISED 1986–1991, 1991–1993, 2000–2004
PLANNER gmp Architekten von Gerkan, Marg und Partner
ADDRESS Flughafenstrasse
ACCESS Open to the public

Thirteen years after the opening of terminal 1, terminal 3 was finished. Both structures are based on competitions won by the Hamburg architectural office gmp. They united the terminal halls to one huge volume correlating in design and static concept and enclosing the much smaller volume of terminal 2. The main characteristic of terminals 1 and 3 are glass façades and tree-shaped pillars bearing the panels of the inclined roof. Based on the research of Frei Otto single limbs transfer the load step by step into the main trunk generating a very delicate and lively image. In terminal 1 twelve tree-pillars are centrally topped by a skylight, arched light-bands cover the interspaces of the single roof panels. Reflectors intensify the incident light. While the roof of terminal 1 traces one continuous curve, the roof of terminal 3 presents a tripartite shed construction supported by eighteen tree-pillars. The realised design connects terminals 1 and 3 at the entrance side in an elegant way. Both halls dock on an apron bar volume that has a trapezoidal cross section, serving the departure and arrival areas as well as the gates.

NEARBY Airport Bus Terminal (2016, wulf architekten, Flughafenstrasse 610)

089

VIEWING PLATFORM KILLESBERG
Killesbergturm

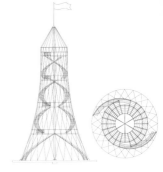

REALISED 2001
PLANNER schlaich bergermann partner, Hans Luz
ADDRESS Höhenpark Killesberg
ACCESS Open to the public

Jörg Schlaich's light and transparent lookout tower on the summit of the
Killesberg was planned for the 1993 International Garden Exhibition, where it
was to mark the end of the intra-urban part of the 'Green U', a greenspace that
connects the city centre with the Killesberg and the woods surrounding the
city. Due to the rising costs of the whole exposition, the city council decided
not to build the tower. At the turn of the millennium the 'Verschönerungs-
verein', an association for the embellishment of Stuttgart, raised the money
to revive and implement the project by selling the right to name each of the
348 steps of the staircases after the donor. The finally realised tower has
four viewing platforms that are stacked around a central mast and stiffened
by covering steel plates. They are embraced by a hypha-shaped cable net
that stabilises the mast and is anchored in a foundation ring. Around most of
the perimeter, the platforms are attached to the end of the joists holding the
cables in position, giving the hypha its form. The construction provides
visitors with a unique experience of height, wind and a panoramic view.

NEARBY 'Die Milchbar' (1950, Rolf Gutbrod, Höhenpark Killesberg)

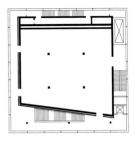

090

ART MUSEUM
Kunstmuseum

REALISED 2002–2005
PLANNER Hascher Jehle Architektur
ADDRESS Kleiner Schlossplatz 1
ACCESS Open to the public

Since the early 1980s, when Günter Behnisch redeveloped Königstrasse as a pedestrian zone, the 'Kleiner Schlossplatz' seemed to be a forgotten space. To fill this void the architects Hascher and Jehle designed a glass cube that completes the corner of the Schlossplatz, filling the gap between Wittwer-Bau (1969, Kammerer + Belz) and Königsbau (Christian Friedrich von Leins, 1860) and BW-Bank (Rolf Gutbrod, 1968) and adding the 'Kleiner Schlossplatz' as part of a sequence of urban squares. The museum is smooth, elegant and reflective. Depending on the incidence of light, the building either looks opaque, semi-transparent or clear. Inside the materials used change from concrete walls and black basalt to white-varnished parquet and white walls in the museum space. 115 m deep relics of a tram tunnel have been transferred to a sequence of two-storey exhibition spaces linked by openings and walkway bridges. In the glass cube's upper levels corridors surround a core of limestone walls providing space for temporary exhibitions. Several openings lead into these spaces, while the glass façade allows the circular view of the surroundings. On the top floor there is a restaurant with a beautiful viewing terrace.

091

INTERNATIONAL CENTRE
Internationales Zentrum (IZ)

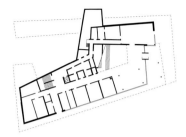

REALISED 2003–2005
PLANNER Dasch Zürn von Scholley
ADDRESS Pfaffenwaldring 60
ACCESS Open to the public

The International Centre sits in the centre of the university campus in Vaihingen, between the student residences and faculty buildings. With its completion in 2005, international students and their German counterparts received a common place to go for help and advice. The three-storey building is characterised by a horizontal convolution of walls and floors visualising their exposed edges and individual sizes at the façade. The fair-faced concrete and glass used for the façade support this contrast. The convolution also becomes apparent in the connected spaces of the interior. The entrance level has a spacious foyer, a meeting place, a cafeteria and an adjacent courtyard. Due to the disposition of the stairs in longitudinal direction they can also be used as an auditorium. The two upper levels contain administration offices, classrooms, language labs and a library. The choice of fair-faced concrete as façade material makes reference to the surrounding buildings. The continuously glazed façade provides an air of brightness and transparency, which, combined with the use of bright colours inside, creates a welcoming atmosphere.

092

MERCEDES-BENZ MUSEUM

REALISED 2004–2006
PLANNER UN studio van Berkel & Bos; Werner Sobek; HG Merz
ADDRESS Mercedesstrasse 100
ACCESS Open to the public

Mercedes Benz has created a gleaming metallic sculpture, a monument to its brand image, its history and above all its automobiles. The entrance of the building is elevated by one storey, raising the museum and its cultural significance above its industrial surroundings. After taking the lift to the eighth floor, the visitors undertake a journey downwards through 120 years of the history of Mercedes Benz. The geometric structure bases on the form of a double helix. The symmetrical layout of the clover-leaf plan is compounded in section by the rotation of the various levels at different heights. The individual clover-leaves, set out around a triangular atrium, form five horizontal planes, each of which consists of single-storey and a two-storey segment. The execution of the difficult geometry of the sculptural design was made possible by in-situ concrete. It was the only material that can be formed into double-curved elements, called 'twists'. The façade of the building is a varied combination of spiral ascending glass strips and concrete columns, tilted inwards to support the different levels.

NEARBY Mercedes Benz Arena (1933/1938/1973/2006, Bonatz & Scholer/ Stuttgart Building Construction Office/Siegel, Wonneberg + Partner/ Arat, Siegel + Partner, Mercedesstrasse 87)

093

CATHEDRAL CHOIR SCHOOL
Domsingschule

REALISED 2005–2006
PLANNER no w here architekten designer
ADDRESS Landhausstrasse 29
ACCESS None

The cubic and plastic moulded volume sitting at the street's edge was built on behalf of Stuttgart's general association of Catholic parishes and is the result of a competition won by Karl Amann and Henning Volpp (founders of no w here). The hermetic four-storey construction displays levels of different height defined by the use and recess of the ochre and beige coloured bricks as the main façade material. White eternit panel surfaces cause sparingly used contrasts. The front façade's ground floor indents, while a slim slab connects the street with the upper frontage. The large rehearsal hall tapers parabolically and twists vertically seeking the connection to the recessed ground floor. Only in the upper two levels an oblong opening interrupts the monolithic brick plain. The building envelope continues the recessed layer, while the gap provides space for terraces and balconies. The structure's plasticity proceeds at the back, but here the frontage's shielded character vanishes into a well-balanced relation of closed and open planes. A two-storey glazed corridor links the main volume with a small rehearsal hall at the rear of the courtyard.

094

WALDORF SCHOOL UHLANDSHÖHE
Waldorfschule Uhlandshöhe

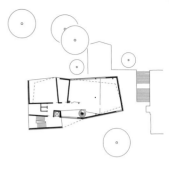

REALISED 2005–2007
PLANNER Aldinger Architekten
ADDRESS Haußmannstrasse 44
ACCESS None

Founded in 1919 by the cigarette producer Emil Molt and named after his brand, the independent Waldorf School Uhlandshöhe marks the beginning of a worldwide growing educational movement. The latest additions were a café, a library and an after-school care club. Accessible through the school campus, the building on four levels has entrances on the ground and garden floors. On the second floor are bedrooms, side rooms and a terrace, on the first floor the library and the computer room and on the main floor the canteen and the activity room, which have a flexible dividing wall. The school building is quite complex in its geometric structure. The floor plan and the façade are a new interpretation of the architectural ideas of Rudolf Steiner, the founder of the anthroposophical philosophy and draughtsman of the Goetheanum (1928) in Dornach. The new design follows the symbolism of a tree-space protected by lightweight and space-wrapping structures. The pile-supported building is characterised by exposed concrete surfaces, wide protruding ceiling slabs and timber-glass elements on its façade, which reflect the geometry of the floor plans. The façade itself is non-bearing and rear-ventilated, which lowers the energy consumption of the building.

095

PORSCHE MUSEUM

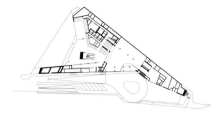

REALISED 2005–2008

PLANNER Delugan Meissl Associated Architects

ADDRESS Porscheplatz

ACCESS Open to the public

The central design concept was to translate Porsche's versatile and vivid brand into a spatial, sensual occurrence. Separated into two main and two basement levels and containing a vertical shaft for lifts and two cores with Y-shaped columns, the museum is an open, clearly defined place. The upper main floors form a dynamic structure called 'Flieger' that emerges in a polygonal shape. It is 160 m in length, weighs 35,000 tons, reaches a max. width spread of 60 m and bases on a steel construction. The building is slightly elevated and accessible via gently dipping steps which lead directly into the foyer, restaurant and museum workshop. Inside, not only the wide-ranging exhibition hall on the upper floors is coloured in white, enabling the visitor to focus on the exhibition items; outside the volume is also clad with white-coated, lozenge-shaped aluminium panels. Much of its sense of weight is relieved by the polished stainless-steel sheeting underneath. The dynamically formed, monolithic structure is seemingly detached from the entry level's folded topography. The museum's reflective soffit absorbs the architectural landscape below.

096

ROOFTOP ADDITION | 40
Dachaufstockung | 40

REALISED 2008–2009
PLANNER Florian Danner
ADDRESS Immenhofer Strasse 40
ACCESS None

A permeable post-war provisional on top of a Wilhelmine block of flats provided the chance for the extravagant solution of project I 40. In accordance with the city's planning laws, the architect Florian Danner developed a folded shell that transforms itself from roof to wall to floor. From the front side it resembles a compressed and entangled S-shape that is recessed from the old building's edge. With its up to 27° inclined glass panes the outer skin roughly follows the outline of a steep roof. Structurally it is a glulam truss construction coated with sprayed light grey polyurethane. This is combined with a bearing steel construction and the concrete extension of the staircase stiffening the whole structure. On a footprint of 98 m² each, its two inversely arranged maisonettes have a living area with kitchen, a separate study and guest toilet on the lower level, while minimalistic cantilevering horizontal steel panels allow access to the bedroom with its open bath zone. The open plan layout and fluid spaces let in lots of light. Inside and outside the roof addition is elegant in appearance and protective in character, as well as very visible.

097

CITY LIBRARY AT MAILÄNDER PLATZ
Stadtbibliothek am Mailänder Platz

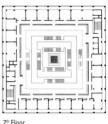

7th Floor

REALISED 2008–2011
PLANNER Eun Young Yi
ADDRESS Mailänder Platz 1
ACCESS Open to the public

At the heart of the new Europaviertel stands the cuboid of the city library. Based on an architectural competition held back in 1999, the design has remained largely unchanged from the competition entry. Measuring 44 m in depth and length and 40 m in height, the building's main material is smooth grey concrete. Glass bricks fill the 81 nearly square openings on each side of the building. Behind this first façade sits a second fully glazed façade with loggias in the front, which can be lit white or blue at night. Visitors enter the building through 'the room of silence' in the middle of the building that spans four of the nine floors with the library spaces around it. A few openings perforate the white walls and a roof light in the middle connects this space without function to the spaces above. The stairs to the upper floor are arranged in-between the 'room of silence' and the library spaces. The main reading hall on the top five floors is funnel-shaped and the spacious middle point of the surrounding spaces. Offices, a cafeteria and other rooms on the top floor offer views of the city.

NEARBY Arcotel Camino (1872, Georg Morlok, 2008, Christoph Mäckler, Heilbronner Strasse 31), Z-UP (2009, Wolfgang Kergaßner, Vordernbergstrasse 6), Milaneo (2014, RKW | Architektur + Städtebau, Mailänder Platz 7)

098

OFFICE BUILDING AT HERDWEG
Bürogebäude am Herdweg

REALISED 2011
PLANNER blocher partners
ADDRESS Herdweg 19
ACCESS None

This cubic office building with four and a half storeys was designed by and for the architects blocher partners in the north of the city. Its L-shape footprint was defined by the former building of the Stuttgart Masonic Lodge. To fit into the urban context the architects reinterpreted the saddle roof and designed a folding roof of exposed concrete elements with two inserted roof terraces. The exposed concrete façade makes reference to the manufacturing process and its surface structure. Ribbon windows and movable wooden mahogany panels define the outer design. Where the façade and the roof meet, a thin metal strip, which is also used as a gutter, marks the transition. Transparency, communication and interaction are the main aspects of the ground floor where the walls are made of movable glass panes. The interior is arranged around two building cores. Open steel stairs connect the floors. In this building design meets sustainability, as the outer walls have core insulation, windows only cover a small surface, LED lights are used and energy is generated geothermally.

NEARBY Linden Museum (1911, Georg Eser, Herdweg 1)

099

HOSPITALHOF STUTTGART
Neubau Hospitalhof

REALISED 2012–2014
PLANNER LRO Lederer Ragnarsdóttir Oei
ADDRESS Büchsenstrasse 33
ACCESS Restricted

The structure of the Hospitalhof goes back to the the 15th century when the hospital church and a Dominican monastery were on the present site. After the Reformation the facilities became the property of the Protestant Church that built a hospital. The complex was destroyed in WW II, except for the south wall of the church and the altar, which later were included in Wolf Irion's redesign of 1961. As these facilities no longer fulfilled the technical requirements, a competition was called and won by LRO in 2009. Like the church, their L-shaped building is slightly skewed to the urban grid, adopting the historical pattern of the monastery buildings. The administration wing extends the church nave. The nave's windows are adapted in a modern shape, connecting the two buildings in their design. Light-coloured brick characterises the outer appearance of the building. French windows on the ground floor remind us of the monastery. Concrete elements shelter round windows in front of the main lecture hall, wooden shutters regulate the influx of daylight. Six trees in the yard symbolise the erstwhile church's columns.

100

STUTTGART CHAMBER OF INDUSTRY AND COMMERCE
Industrie- und Handelskammer (IHK) Region Stuttgart

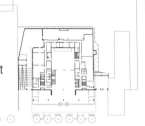

REALISED 2012–2014
PLANNER wulf architekten
ADDRESS Jägerstrasse 30
ACCESS Restricted

The new compact and U-shaped building of the regional headquarters of the Stuttgart Chamber of Industry and Commerce opens up at the rear to one of the vineyards that are characteristic of Stuttgart, while—at the front—it creates a clear edge. Wall-high glass elements characterise the recessed, transparent entrance area. This light structure is topped by a protruding cuboid, structured by pilaster strips lending a depth and verticality to the façade. The first three floors are public spaces, including a big foyer, connected to a lecture hall, conference rooms of different sizes and a cafeteria facing the vineyard. The upper floors house office spaces. The U-shaped floor plan allows desks to be placed in front of the windows. The zones between the work-spaces are for storage, meetings or additional working space. As the layout is mostly open plan and windows are high, daylight floods the building. Far from looking glazed, the plastered surfaces, exposed concrete walls and natural materials give the building a warm atmosphere that is further enhanced by the sound-absorbing fleece in the colourful panels that guide visitors.

NEARBY School of Public Administration (1971, Rolf Gutbier, Jägerstrasse 58)

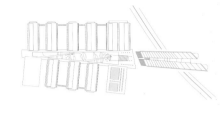

NEW TRADE FAIR COMPLEX
Neue Messe

REALISED 2004–2007; 2016–2017
PLANNER wulf architekten
ADDRESS Messepiazza 1
ACCESS Open to the public

One of the principal design concepts for the New Trade Fair Complex was the alignment in east-west direction, a multi-storey car park serving as a landscape bridge spanning over the motorway and a scaling of the eight exhibition halls and a congress centre in different heights. The facility forms a connected urban context interacting with the nearby airport in Leinfelden-Echterdingen. All buildings are aligned along a main circulation path with the two main entrances at its respective ends. Seven of the eight exhibition halls are standardised, one is of a larger type for hosting special events. The largest hall mirrors two standard type halls at their centreline, both suspension roofs combined with a space truss span an unsupported area of 140 m × 140 m. The multi-storey car park, designed as a so-called 'green wave', connects it to the surrounding landscape by spanning across the motorway and the railway line. The façades as well as the whole architectural design of the buildings are transparent, displaying all the constructional aspects of the buildings and representing the form and main principles of the design itself. A new hall was added to the trade fair complex in 2017.

REGISTER ARCHITECTS